GETTING CONNECTED

HOW TO IMPROVE ALL
YOUR RELATIONSHIPS

GETTING CONNECTED
How To Improve All Your Relationships

Published in 1999 by William Boyle & Associates.
Second Printing 2001

Designed and printed in the United States
by Elk Grove Graphics, Elk Grove Village, IL

Distributed by William Boyle & Associates
P.O. Box 92048
Elk Grove Village, IL 60009-2048

ISBN 0-9675289-0-9

CONTENTS

DEDICATION

This book is dedicated to four of the most special people in my life: my Mother, my Father, and my twin sons, Michael and Matthew.

During my lifetime, I have had many teachers. Most of them taught me how to think, write, speak, study, and learn. But only one teacher instructed me in the fine arts of love, acceptance, and forgiveness, and that is my Mother. While others taught me how to <u>DO</u>, Mom taught me how to <u>BE</u>. It is because of her loving care and guidance, and her thousands of prayers for me over many years, that I have been able to successfully navigate my way through life for 52 years. She is actually the inspiration for this book, and so I dedicate it to her. As I have told her on numerous occasions, in the words of the popular song, "You are the wind beneath my wings."

I dedicate this book to my Father because without his work ethic influence, and his insistence upon honesty and integrity, I would have very little to write about. My Dad has always been a paragon of a model man—consistently doing what he believed was right, regardless of circumstances or consequences. It is unfortunate that, because of his recent death, he will be unable to read the book. But he will always be an inspiration to me, and I will always know that my growth in life so far is due to his behavioral modeling.

My son Michael is one of the most delightful young men one could ever meet. He is clever and spontaneous, quite unlike his father. He is a deep thinker, always asking questions and wondering why things work the way they do. He loves to figure out the answers to riddles, games, and blue prints. I dedicate this book to him because I want him to realize exactly where I am on my journey through life, and I want him to commit himself to continue living life the way he has done so for almost 19 years. He inspires me far more than he knows.

My son Matthew loves life as much as anyone else I have ever met. One of my most favorite sounds is Matthew laughing at something he thinks is very funny. He is tenacious in everything he does. When he works, he works harder than the people around him. If there is a way to beat an opponent in a game, he will find it. I dedicate this book to him because I want him to understand how important people are in my life, and I want him to commit to continue living his life with as much caring for others as he has always demonstrated. Like his brother, he inspires me more than he knows.

I dedicate this book to my Mother, my Father, Michael, and Matthew—four of the most intimate relationship partners one could ever hope to have. I am blessed!

William Boyle
July 1999

ACKNOWLEDGMENTS

I have had considerable assistance in writing this book, mainly through life experiences. In that regard, the people who deserve thanks are too numerous to mention by name, but they have all affected my life in some way. As a group, I would like to mention my hundreds of adult students who I have taught over the past 20 years. I continue to learn from them on a weekly basis, and I treasure the wonderful times we have shared, learning together. In particular, three groups of students deserve special recognition—Urban 101, Urban 102, and Elgin 37. These students utilized the manuscript in two classes, and provided me with greatly-appreciated feedback. Special gratitude goes to Dezire Gordon and Karen Hobik, who corrected some significant typos for me, and also to Amy MacTavish from Elk Grove Graphics who designed and created this book.

My fellow faculty members were of tremendous assistance, as they read my manuscript, and offered helpful suggestions. I am most grateful to them: Marylee Darr, Flo Galloway, Bill Graham, Nancy Gup, Lynette LaHay, Natalie Manbeck, Aloma Mendoza, Debbie O'Reilly, Shirley Weiglein.

Three good friends assisted me by proofreading the manuscript, supplying me with ideas, and offering continuous support. They are dear friends who I greatly love. Thank you Jim Campain, Elly Clark, and Kathy Schweigert.

I would like to offer special thanks to two individuals who have been most helpful to me. They have proofread material, offered suggestions to clarify certain concepts, supported me on an almost daily basis, assisted me with graphics, pagination, and other mechanical details. Most of all, these individuals are treasured YOUs in my life (you'll have to read the book to know what that means), and they have supported me in my efforts. I consider them intimate friends, and my special gratitude and love go out to them. They are my treasured soul mates. Thank you Bill Owen and Terry Trietsch. I love you more than I can say.

CREDITS

In this book, I have referred to several other works.
Their bibliographical specifics are as follows:

Augsburger, David. *Caring Enough To Confront*. Glendale, California: Regal Books Division, G/L Publications, 1978.

Patton, Bobby R.; Giffin, Kim; Patton, Eleanor Nyquist. *Decision-Making Group Interaction*. Third Edition. New York: Harper & Row, Publishers, 1989.

Williams, Margery. *The Velveteen Rabbit*. New York: Doubleday & Company, Inc. Date unknown.

This book contains numerous quotes. Those quoted by other individuals are cited as such. Where there is no citation, either the quote source is unknown or is original with this author. Most of the quotes cited were taken from three sources, which are:

Bartlett, John. *Familiar Quotations*. Boston: Little, Brown and Company, 1968.

Cory, Lloyd. *Quote Unquote*. Wheaton, Illinois: Victor Books, 1977.

Quotable Quotes. Pleasantville, New York: The Reader's Digest Association, Inc., 1997.

INTRODUCTION

Just before he went to bed one night, Tony read a chapter in a book which informed him that during the next day he would deal with (either directly or indirectly) literally thousands of people. The awesome thought so intrigued him that, over coffee early the next morning, Tony made a mental list of all the individuals he would encounter that day, in some fashion. He already had spoken with his wife and oldest son, who took an early morning bus to work. He let out the dog, but that doesn't count. He realized that on the train to work, he would be in a car with about 70 other people (after waiting at the station with about 200 others), and that on the short walk to his office, he would say "Good Morning" to the newspaperman, the traffic police person, and six or seven other pedestrians who he would recognize. In addition, he would pass at least several hundred other people.

In the office, Tony would speak briefly with at least 25 other co-workers, meet with 10-15 others, talk on the phone with 20-30 salespeople and colleagues, and deliver a report to about 75 directors. At his Rotary meeting luncheon, he would mingle with about 200 other Rotarians, and he would eat food prepared and served by several dozen employees of the hotel. During the afternoon, Tony would sign a contract which included input from at least 50 other people at three different companies, not to mention those who had provided clerical assistance. He attempted to estimate how many individuals contributed to the newspaper he would buy and read, but at that hour of the morning, it was a futile task.

After work, Tony would ride the commuter train home, eat dinner that had been purchased from the local grocery store (with dozens of employees and hundreds of suppliers), and attend his youngest son's baseball game, along with about 30 ball players, 40 parents and coaches, and one umpire. Later in the evening, Tony would watch the ten o'clock news, and a few minutes of the late night talk show, both of which involved several hundreds of television employees. "Wow," Tony thought, "that book was pretty accurate. It seems the only person on earth that I won't deal with today is the Chairman of the Federal Reserve." Then he turned on the radio and heard that the interest rates were going up another percentage point.

> ## *"No man is an island."*
> ## *– John Donne*

This is a book about relationships, and it covers the full gamut. We will talk about ourselves, people we know well, people we know not-so-well, and people we do not know at all and never will. That pretty much covers the entire universe. But I am suggesting that we have some kind of relationship with every human being on this particular planet, and that is why I have chosen to include all of them in our discussion. You may be married or have a significant other in your life, you may have children, you definitely have relatives somewhere, you may have living parents or grandparents, you have neighbors, you have people with whom you work or interact on a regular basis, you have people you pass on the street every day, you have people you read about or see on TV, and you have fellow human beings around the globe. First and foremost, you have yourself, and therefore you have relationships.

Many of us take our relationships for granted, and we do not spend much time thinking about them. We don't analyze them to see if they are effective or might need improvement. We don't take the time to notice the strengths and weaknesses of our relationships. Sometimes when the relationship is severely lacking, we passively assume that it will always be that way, and it is no use attempting to change it for the better. Sometimes we confuse the word "relationship" with peaceful (or not-so-peaceful) coexistence. In some cases, we may not even know what a true relationship is like because we have never experienced a healthy one, not even with our own families when we were growing up. It is my hope that in this book, we will understand what relationships are all about, we will comprehend what goes into developing and maintaining and growing a relationship, and we will actively pursue meaningful relationships which will enhance our lives significantly.

The book is divided into four sections, titled "ME," "YOU," "US," "THEM." We will start with <u>ME</u> because, as is explained in detail in the first chapter, if I cannot relate to myself, I have no hope of ever relating to any other person in a mature or meaning fashion. We will then discuss <u>YOU</u>, and we will quickly learn that these are people with whom we have a very special relationship. <u>US</u> refers to the relationship between ME and YOU, where two people basically become one in spirit. Finally, we will talk about <u>THEM</u>, all the other people in our lives and in the world.

WHY DID I WRITE THIS BOOK?

I don't know about you, but whenever I pick up a book of this type, I always question the author's credentials and motives. I ask questions like: How inflated must her ego be to assume that she has something to teach me? Why does he think he knows more than I do about this topic? Does she think that just because she has a degree behind her name that she is an expert and I should read what she has written? Is he really convinced that he has something worthwhile to share, or is he merely trying to make a dollar at my expense?

Let me respond to those questions. As I will state several times in the book and again in the Conclusion, I do not pretend to have all the answers when it comes to maintaining effective relationships. I have made numerous relational mistakes in my life, and I continue to do so. I am a fellow struggler with you in this crucial arena of life. I wish I could say that I have found the magic potion of relational living, but I have not. I fight the same battles that you do on a daily basis, and I do not have the textbook remedies that all of us want in order to perfect our relationships.

This admission elicits bad news and good news. The bad news is that if you are looking for "the answer" to every relational problem or concern, then you are holding the wrong book. Please give it to someone else, and resume your quest for the panacea we all need. Unfortunately, it is not available anywhere. The good news is that since I am a fellow struggler, I am able to offer some ideas and suggestions which have been extremely helpful to me, which have served me well in my efforts to improve all of my relationships. Since I have committed myself to life-long learning, I have made a conscious attempt to benefit from past mistakes and failures. This book is a summary of my learnings so far on the road to effective relationships.

If you wanted to speak with someone about problems you were having with your son or daughter, would you talk to another parent, or would you talk with someone who had never had children? If you wanted counsel about an addictive habit you have, would you prefer to speak with someone who was recovering from that problem, or would you prefer to talk to someone who had never experienced the difficulty? If you wanted to get along better with your boss, lose weight, better manage your time, or buy a particular model of car, with whom would you speak?

I have written this book because I sense that there are many thousands of people who need to re-examine their relationship patterns, just as I do. There are countless individuals who want desperately to experience positive and meaningful relationships in their lives, just as I do. I offer the ideas and suggestions in this book because they work for me, and I think they can work for almost everyone who truly desires to grow and mature and succeed in his or her relational world.

WHO SHOULD READ THIS BOOK?

Anyone taking a course for which this book is required reading, and who will have a test over it, should definitely read the book. Other than that, I would recommend it only to those who have relationships, and who would like to see them improve, grow, and mature. Hopefully, that is all of us. I would like to better understand myself, I would like to better appreciate my intimate relationship partners, I would like to better celebrate the special bonds we have with each other, and I would like to better accept and value all the other people who share "humanness" with me.

Your situation may be different from Tony's, and maybe you do not have as many overt "relationships" as he does, but if you were to pause and list all the unknown people with whom you interact on a daily basis (directly or indirectly), it might shock you. In this book, I am suggesting that we have some kind of relationship with all these people, as well as with the millions of others who we will never meet or encounter in any way.

As I will suggest in the last section of the book, most of us have the opportunity to influence numerous people every day, either positively or negatively. We have a chance to "make their day" or "break their day." I have some ideas to offer which I think can help us to concentrate on the positive aspects of ourselves and others, and which can assist us in improving all the relationships in our lives. I trust you will find this book to be inspiring, invigorating, and enlightening, but most of all useful as you embark on one of the noblest of all paths—the building and continuous growth of relationships.

PART 1

CHAPTER I

◆◆◆

MIRROR, MIRROR, ON THE WALL

"Know Thyself"
The Oracle at Delphi

The older I get, the more I appreciate the value of that simple two-word admonition from The Oracle at Delphi, "Know Thyself." To me, it is the essential first ingredient in the recipe for success in living and in relationships. If I do not truly know myself, I can never hope to effectively set my goals, chart my life, or evaluate my progress and success. If I do not realistically understand who I am, or why I am the way that I am, how can I possibly understand who you are? How can I make sense of our differences, and appreciate you for bringing variety into my life? If I maintain a naïve and superficial understanding of myself, I will blindly assume my own superiority, and I will judge you to be in error when it comes to differences in our temperaments, attitudes, beliefs, and behaviors.

The longest journey begins with one step.

An ancient adage states, "The longest journey begins with one step." Likewise, the understanding of our world begins with the understanding of ourselves. If I try to make sense of the world without first understanding myself, I make a fatal mistake because I do not realize how biased my perceptions are. I equate my "tunnel vision" with reality, and my actions with correct behavior. Anything outside of my immediate sphere of intention or activity is dismissed as abnormal or improper, because until I gain insight into myself, I cannot appreciate that differences are natural and healthy and necessary in a complex world.

Can I understand what it is like to go through life as a blind person, or a person of a different race, or gender? Not really, because I have never been there. However, if I introspectively attempt to understand who I am, then I am capable of gaining insight as to how it might be to be different from the way I am. Through repeated honest inquiry, I can grasp the reality of my uniqueness, complete with my own temperament, tendencies, biases, and values. Then, and only then, can I begin to understand and accept others in a positive light.

There were many times earlier in my life when I found it impossible to understand why colleagues and associates said some of the things they said, and did some of the things they did. The unhappy fact is that I did not try to understand who they were and why they thought differently from me. Unaware of myself, I ignorantly and unconsciously assumed that I was normal, and that others were out of step with the world. To gain an accurate and meaningful perception of anything outside of myself, I first must truly understand myself.

Two Pitfalls

I see two pitfalls here. The first is to disregard knowledge of self, to render it non-essential, and to dive headlong into the quest for a meaningful life, and effective relationships. That is like attempting algebra before mastering addition. It is tantamount to trying to create a symphony prior to understanding basic scale. It is equivalent to thinking about jumping hurdles before learning to walk. To ignore the understanding of self is to guarantee failure at attempting to relate to others, or to develop a life plan.

The second pitfall is more dangerous and insidious, because it is more subtle and difficult to detect. This is the assumption that one has already mastered the understanding of self, when it is in fact a mistaken assumption. When one blithely assumes that he or she has self-understanding (when that is not really the case), results are usually devastating, because the person bases decisions and actions on invalid information. This person speeds down the track unhindered, but has boarded the wrong train. It would be like a detective mis-reading a piece of evidence, and basing a deductive theory on the mistake. All the procedures may be followed flawlessly and diligently, but if the initial premise is wrong, the final diagnosis is meaningless at best, and damaging or fatal at worst.

This second scenario typically occurs because a person naively equates experience with learning. For example, because I have lived a number of years with myself, I assume that I truly understand who I am and what I am all about. I know my tendencies, attitudes, beliefs, concerns, likes and dislikes, talents, dreams, limitations, and methods of operating; therefore, I must really know myself. Unfortunately, that is not always the case. We can only truly know ourselves when we take the time to regularly "reflect" on ourselves, and to honestly analyze and evaluate who we are and why we are that way. This requires sincere reflection. Socrates proclaimed, "The unexamined life is not worth living." I would add that the unexamined life certainly places one in a position where he or she can never understand other people, and can never maintain a healthy and meaningful relationship.

Do you remember that old expression, "Those who can't do, teach. And those who can't teach, teach others?" (When I taught elementary school, we had a cruel addendum—"Those who can't teach anyone go into administration.") Unfortunately, this expression sometimes holds true. When some people discover they are incapable of performing, they prefer to vacate the quest, and instead attempt to teach others how to perform. When I was in graduate school, I taught undergraduate students part-time for the university, and I shared an office with a professor. One day he told me that he had taught junior high school at one time, but that he could not maintain discipline, and the kids literally drove him out of the school (and ultimately out of teaching at that level). At that point, he completed a doctoral program so that he could instruct others how to teach junior high. It was an incredulous story to hear, but what made it even more bizarre was that he told it with such pride, as if he had found a way to beat the system. His philosophy was that if you find that you are incapable as a "doer," never fear, you can always impart knowledge to others.

This is analogous to the person who does not understand him or her self, but attempts to understand others and pass judgment on their behavior. Without the understanding of self, there is no measuring rod to interpret how others live, there is no basis of comparison, and there is no way to value and appreciate differences.

The Fear of Knowing

I would be remiss if I did not mention that there is a potential scariness about understanding who I really am. Many people don't want to understand themselves for fear of what they might uncover. The psychologist Alfred Adler asserted that one of the first awarenesses we have of ourselves is that of inferiority. Not a comforting thought, is it? In my experience, I have discovered that a significant number of people tend to devalue themselves, to look at themselves as less than acceptable, to reject self-scrutiny because of the potential vulnerability. It is not my intent here to deal with this quasi-clinical issue. Rather, I am suggesting that there are any number of ways of looking at self that are objective, positive, and ecstatically enlightening.

Rather than looking at myself in order to detect my shortcomings, I want to gain a clearer understanding of the "type" of person I am. I want to discover my temperament, understand my attitudes, realize my talents, and clarify my values. I want to know how I am wired up, so that I can appreciate my preferences and tendencies, and know why I react as I do to other people and situations. I want to eliminate my fear of knowing who I am by focusing on the reality of my positive self, by realizing that I am "OK" just the way I am, by concentrating on the true me (and not the me that I assume I am or wish I were). At that point I can assess how I like the "me" that I am, and attempt to make adjustments where I feel it is appropriate.

Self-Assessment Activity

As I stated a few sentences ago, there are a myriad of ways of looking at myself that are positive, enlightening, and eye-opening. There are any number of methods of self-scrutiny that will reveal to me who I am, and once I attain that knowledge, I will be better able to assess myself in light of how others differ from me. Let me mention just a few exercises that will assist in the discovery of self.

I. SNAPSHOT

First, take a physical snapshot of yourself. Look at who you are on the surface. Look at your skin tone, your muscular structure, your proportions, your pleasant and unpleasant features. What do you like?

What would you like to change? Try to observe yourself from your own perspective—ignore what others have said about you. Chances are others have commented only on your "beautiful features", as we typically avoid relating to others what we don't like. What do you like? Do you belittle yourself because of a physical blemish or scar? Does that pre-empt every other pleasant physical feature about you? If so, is that the first thing you notice about other people? Do they appear to you as unattractive?

Now, take a psychological snapshot of yourself. What is unique about you, something that sets you apart from others? What are your values? What are your goals? What is the first impression you make on others as you interact with them? What does the snapshot look like when you observe yourself?

2. THIS IS ME

Second, complete a "This Is Me" inventory. Discover more about who you are by writing sentences or phrases about your character, abilities, attitudes, desires, potentials, perceptions, etc. For example, you might want to complete sentences such as:

> I am good at . . .
>
> I am proud of . . .
>
> I like people who are . . .
>
> One thing I need is . . .
>
> I have the potential to . . .

As you concentrate on specific characteristics and areas such as those listed above, you will gain significant insight as to who you really are, and you can understand yourself from many different dimensions. Hang a mental mobile of yourself from the ceiling, and then walk around the room, looking at yourself from several different angles. Admire yourself as a total person: physically, emotionally, psychologically, spiritually, educationally. Applaud your special talents. Bask in your more spectacular successes.

> ## *"I yam what I yam."*
> ## *– Popeye*

Note your weaknesses (are they crucial from your perspective, or inconsequential?). Salute your dreams. Consider your values—do you really live by them, or are they merely given lip-service? If they appear to be alien, then ask whether they are truly your own values, or ones that have been imposed on you at one time or another. If you verbalize them as values, but discover that your behavior is not consistent with them, then maybe they need to be exposed as interlopers, and replaced with those things that are <u>really</u> your values. Do you see how such scrutiny of yourself could possibly give you insight as you attempt to interact with others? Is it beginning to make sense that the only way to understand the intricacies and complexities of the world is first to be certain that my own self is not playing tricks on me? And if I can say that "This Is Me" in a multi-faceted manner, isn't that better than responding to the question, "Who are you?" by saying, "I'm Arlene, a 37 year-old seamstress from Duluth?"

3. CATERPILLAR - BUTTERFLY

This one is very simple to understand, yet extremely difficult to perform. The concept is not profound, but the execution requires a great deal of skill. Most of all, it requires mature reflection, and it assumes that significant growth has taken place in one's life over a number of years. If that is not the case, that is okay, as long as it is recognized. In other words, if I have not grown intellectually and emotionally since I was young, that is not disastrous, as long as I realize what I can yet do to stimulate that growth. As I have told my adult students continuously over many years, "It is not wrong to make mistakes; it is only wrong to not know that you have made mistakes." If I know that I am wrong, I can make adjustments. If I recognize the flaw, I can correct it. If I look in the mirror and discover that I shaved only the right side of my face, then I am capable of making the left side just as smooth. But if I pay no attention to the reflection, then I appear grotesque (especially after a week or so), although it is my understanding that people with physical or psychological "grotesqueness" make a fortune by appearing on TV talk shows.

The key here is the recognition of my growth status. How much have I matured over the past several years? Am I the same person today that I was ten or fifteen years ago? Do I view things exactly the same way now as I did when I was younger, with less experience and maturity? Have I altered my attitudes, paradigms, and perceptions based on my growth, or have I merely maintained my status quo? Have I confused experience with learning? By that I mean, have I assumed that by experiencing many things, I have learned from them? Have I lived the past 10 years, or have I lived the past year 10 times? Have I equated the quantity of life (years) with the quality of life (learning)?

When I taught elementary school, we had a fourth-grade teacher who bragged that she had not altered a lesson plan in years. In her opinion, what was good in 1965 was also good in 1975, if not better. Kids were still kids to her, curriculum was still curriculum, discipline was still discipline. On occasions, I wanted to ask her what she would think if her paycheck remained the same for ten years, with no increases for inflation, since nothing ever changes. I refrained, since I was young, untenured, and smaller than she was. Incidentally, I was still teaching in 1971 with a science book that proclaimed that someday man would walk on the moon (which occurred on July 20, 1969). Oh well, you can't be current on everything.

Young children do not understand that a caterpillar eventually becomes a butterfly. How can this creepy, crawly, furry creature evolve into a multi-colored flying phenomenon? With apologies to caterpillars, how can this limited land-bound insect blossom into a soaring dream that brings beauty wherever it lands? The answer lies in the maturing process, the metamorphosis which takes place over time. Make no mistake, the caterpillar is not ugly. It is a beautiful creature in infancy, just as children are one of creation's most breathtakingly gorgeous products. It exhibits the beauty of innocence and curiosity, and it moves at glacial speed, savoring each step along its cautious path. As it sheds its "no longer needed" skin, it sprouts wings, and it soars above the ground it used to tread, affording it a perspective which it could have never realized before. It revolutionizes its view of reality, and it totally alters its understanding of the world in which it exists. The analogy to children is ridiculously obvious. As they escape the land-bound territory of home influence, they anticipate the unexpected, and they crave the unfamiliar. They thrive on that which is challenging and slightly beyond their reach.

I used to be very quick to judge gay men because of their sexual orientation. I was a product of my upbringing, I believed they were wrong, and I felt quite self-righteous about it. Then I knew a gay man who died of AIDS, and I became friends with several other gay men, whom I admired because of their exuberance, their acceptance of others, and their positive outlook on life. My caterpillar began to evolve. I began to view gay men from a different perspective, at least the ones I knew. I eschewed my judgment, and opted instead for a perspective of acceptance, without prejudice.

Slowly, I began to realize that while I do not endorse a life-style of homosexuality (which I cannot truly understand, never having had those tendencies), what right do I have to label my friends or associates? Am I better than they are? Even if I do not personally approve of their lifestyle, is it worse than my tendency to criticize, blame, or judge others?

Does my more mature "butterfly" outlook on life allow me the freedom to perceive situations in a different light than I used to when I identified with the caterpillar? I hope so, because the butterfly surveys the terrain from above, as opposed to from the surface. It enjoys a panorama that cannot be experienced from the ground. Think about the last time you flew in an airplane over a large city like New York or Chicago. Do you remember how different the perspective was from when you drove through the same city on an expressway? Admittedly, part of that variance might have been due to the fact that when you were driving, your eyes were glued to the traffic in your quest for survival, but the point should be obvious. The butterfly has a perspective that is far more advantageous than the one of the caterpillar.

Using the caterpillar-butterfly scenario, think about some important issues in your personal or professional life where you have experienced significant change due to the maturing process (similar to my change of perspective on gay men). This is another way of looking at yourself to analyze your growth and progress, and to celebrate your "process of metamorphosis." What are some areas of your life that represent significant growth in perspective? Relationships with friends? Understanding of co-workers? Tolerance of different personalities? Learning to forgive? Reflect on some of your successes in "perspective-change," and then list several other areas where you feel the need to make adjustments. Can you apply some of the same principles from your successes in order to increase your butterfly abilities?

4. BRAG SESSION

If you grew up like I did, you were taught to never brag. Bragging is bad. Nobody likes braggarts. They are obnoxious, boorish, and self-centered. They never want to talk about you—they only want to talk about themselves. They think they have no faults. The thing that used to bother me most was that braggarts always seemed to have a good reason to boast—they <u>were</u> good at most things. As one well-known athlete commented, "It ain't bragging if you can do it." But nevertheless, polite society teaches that it is impolite to brag. In fact, there is a Bible verse that states, "Let another man praise thee, and not thine own self."

I tend to agree with the above sentiments. I have a hard time with braggarts. I prefer humble people who attribute their successes to others who have made a contribution to their lives. Psychologically, I find braggarts to be insecure people who need attention or stroking in order to feel okay about themselves. I also observe many of them to be "truth-stretchers." Even the most talented braggart runs out of impressive stories and statistics about him or her self, and has to rely on creative fiction to maintain the image of superiority.

Do you remember the Saturday Night Live skit featuring the pathological liar? He was the one who would always take credit for achieving a magnificent feat, or accomplishing the impossible task. If someone mentioned the Gettysburg address, he would respond something like this: "Yeah, I remember that. In fact, I <u>wrote</u> that. Yeah, that's it. I wrote that." Or when he saw the Empire State Building, he might comment, "What a great building. I've been there. Actually, I go there every day. Come to think of it, I <u>own</u> it. Yeah, I own that building. In fact, I own the entire block around it. Yeah, it all belongs to me." The pathological liar tended to be an extreme case of a braggart, but I have known several people in my lifetime who exhibit similar tendencies, although in a somewhat more subtle manner.

> *"I'm a very good man.*
> *I'm just a very bad wizard."*
> *– The Wizard of Oz*

So, if I disdain braggarts, why am I suggesting a "Brag Session" as a way of gaining more knowledge about myself? Quite simply, a brag session gives me an opportunity to reflect on some of the things I am good at, or some of the accomplishments in my life that have bolstered my morale and made me feel good about myself. A brag session allows me to realize that I have had many successes in life, and that with hard work and determination, I can have many more. It gives me yet another perspective in the quest to discover who I really am. It helps me to concentrate on talents I possess, which should be utilized on a regular basis; and it also reminds me that some of my successes are truly in the past, and can never be duplicated.

Let me illustrate. Two items on my brag session list are:

1. I was President of my senior class in both high school and college.
2. I was an excellent center-fielder in my softball days, covering so much territory that I earned the nickname "the blanket." (Or maybe it was because they thought I was asleep out there).

With regard to the first item, it suggests that I have always possessed some leadership skills, which I have used on numerous occasions, and can draw upon in the future as opportunities arise. When it comes to the second item, wisdom (not to mention fatigue, back pain, and deterioration of speed) tells me that I will never again appear in a starring role in competitive softball. The brag session gives me a realistic perspective on my talents and abilities, and it helps me to know what I should concentrate on, and what is better left to fond memories. Incidentally, when you bat as poorly as I did, you'd better be pretty good as a fielder, or you will do serious time on the bench.

So, what would you include in your brag session (and if you are still uncomfortable with the word "brag," use an alternative word or expression, such as "positive self-recognition")? Are you artistic? Are you a good cook? Do people value your advice or counsel? Can you build a deck on the back of your house? Can you fly an airplane? Are you proficient with numbers? Do you possess a trophy or medal for an athletic feat? Have you maintained a successful marriage for 40 years? Have you been recognized for perfect attendance at work? Are you a whiz on the computer? What would you include in your brag session? What do your items tell you about yourself?

5. GOAL SETTING

Another way of assessing who you are is to set your sights on your goals and objectives. What is it you would like to accomplish in the next few weeks, months, and years? Or what would you like to <u>become</u> over the same time-frame? The goals you have (if any) will reveal a great deal about you to yourself. I say "if any" because there are people who are devoid of ambition, who have no hope or vision, who exist each day as automatons, eagerly anticipating the next soap opera or sit-com (if they are self-sustaining; otherwise, they anticipate the next meal). It is a pathetically depressing condition, but reality tells us that it exists in regrettably huge numbers. Hopefully, no one reading this has succumbed to the "dream-burglar" who wishes to snatch the life out of life. It is my hope that all of us, regardless of previous successes or failures or bad breaks or disappointments, hold fast to our visions, hopes, dreams, and goals. What is life worth, if not for opportunity and challenge? Why continue to strive if there is no goal to be reached? Frank Sinatra once quipped, "I feel sorry for people who don't drink, because when they wake up in the morning, that's the best they will feel all day." Of course, he was joking, but the humor is not without a message. Those who wake up in the morning without a goal to be reached or a dream to be realized that day are to be pitied. We all have bulls-eyes on the horizon; some people are handed more arrows, while others have to hunt for their own. But there are many to be found by those who visualize the goal and insist on nailing the target.

Goal setting is an excellent way to realize who you are. For one thing, it reveals what you think of yourself and your abilities. When I taught sixth grade in elementary school, I invented a game which I played with my students from time to time. I placed the industrial sized waste basket in the front of the room, and the students attempted to throw a nerf ball into the basket from different distances (believe it or not, this was actually quite educational). They could shoot from five different distances, ranging from very close to very far away. My students with the lowest self-concepts (and poorest academic performances) chose to shoot from extremely close or extremely far away, while the more confident and secure students tended to shoot from the third or fourth distances. This indicated to me that the students with the least self-esteem needed to be successful (shooting from the "gimme" range), or they shot from the range where their misses were expected (of course I missed—no one can make it from here). The students with greater self-esteem chose a range that was challenging, yet possible. They wanted to attempt something reachable, yet they were not afraid to miss.

As we contemplate setting goals, we demonstrate to ourselves who we are. Are the goals too easy? Reachable? Too impossible? Are they challenging without being unrealistic? Are you trying to break a 15-year habit in one day? Are you determined to improve "D" grades to "A"s overnight? Think about the goals you have right now. I would suggest asking yourself the following questions:

1. What is one specific goal I have over the next 3, 6, or 12 months?
2. What resources do I need to attain that goal?
3. What problems or obstacles am I likely to face?
4. How can I overcome these?
5. What schedule will I need to maintain to reach my goal?
6. Who can I count on for assistance in reaching my goal?
7. How will I reward myself when I reach the goal?

Goal setting helps us to look at who we are; what our priorities are, what our determination level is, what we consider success, what our self-esteem level is, and how serious we are to attain goals. Above all, goal setting helps us to focus on opportunities and challenges which lie ahead.

6. WHAT SATISFIES ME?

I was in high school during the 60s, one of the most interesting and memorable eras in American history. Among the innumerable changes which occurred in society was an alteration of popular music, produced (ironically) by British groups. One extremely popular group was the Rolling Stones, although they were overshadowed by the other guys named John, Paul, George, and the drummer with all the rings. At any rate, the Rolling Stones had a monstrous hit called, "I Can't Get No Satisfaction," a tune which appalled parents and English teachers. Although rock music has always been considered pop culture, it epitomized an attitude on the part of many young people of that decade. Discovering satisfaction had become an extremely difficult thing to do. I am not a sociologist, and will not attempt to compare the 60s crowd with earlier generations, although I personally believe that it was during these years that young people began to concentrate more on their own satisfaction (choices, opportunities) than did their predecessors, who were more programmed to focus on assumed roles (duties, obligations). Regardless, the song was a young man's lamentation of the futility of life, in terms of listening to media hype, keeping up with the Joneses, and chasing girls.

Understanding what satisfies me tells me a great deal about myself. You might want to think of several ways to complete this sentence: "I'll be satisfied when . . ." Your responses may deal with possessions, relationships, leisure, health, politics, or any number of other areas. The key here is to honestly assess your responses, and maybe to ask questions like the following: Are these desires attainable or realistic (if not, I have set myself up for eternal dissatisfaction—kind of an emotional death wish)? Are these desires strictly self-centered? If so, what does that say about me? Do all of my desires tend to center around the same theme (relationships, for example)? What does that tell me about my values, what is really important to me? Do my desires all tend to center around the idea of escaping my present situation (I'll be satisfied when I can quit my job, get divorced, see my kids off to college, sell my business, murder my worst clients, etc)? What does that tell me about the way I view myself and my life?

"We would often be sorry if our wishes were gratified."
– Aesop
The Old Man and Death
(quoted in Familiar Quotations, p. 76)

When I was in college, I worked a summer job in construction, as did many of you reading this (there seems to be something un-American about a male college student not working construction during the summer). My immediate supervisor was one of the most miserable human beings I have ever met. He seemingly hated everyone all at once, and maintained a scowl and an intimidating manner for all of us, his "boys." While I disliked him personally, I admired his tenacity and work ethic, and I made him my project for the summer. At no time would I give him cause for criticizing me or belittling me. I would work as hard as he did, and be as tough as he was, yet without emulating his obnoxious manner. I was just one of his "scumbags" until one day things changed. He and I were loading heavy pipes onto the bed of a truck, which was about four feet off the ground. He became irate at something or someone (I honestly don't remember which), and he stomped off, uttering a stream of profanities that would have spanned the Grand Canyon.

Partly because I was angry with him, and partly because I can also be obnoxious, I started loading the remaining pipes, inch by inch, onto the truck by myself. When I completed the task, I sat down to rest, secretly hoping that I would die so as to avoid the certain consequences of spending months in traction. After his anger had subsided long enough for him to once again resemble a human being, he approached me and asked why I had done such a stupid thing as to load the pipes myself instead of waiting for him to return. Feeling pretty good about myself by this time, and knowing that he had gained a certain admiration for me, I replied by saying something that a wiser man would not have offered—I said something like, "Somebody had to finish the job."

Incredibly, it worked! While we did not become friends (I actually believe he was incapable of friendship, and I certainly did not want to hang around with him), we did form a relationship that he shared with no other "scumbag." He began to ask me to assist him with more difficult tasks, and best of all, he quit checking up on me regularly. He knew I was consistently giving my best effort.

One day we were working together, and it began to rain so hard that we had to stop work for a while and sit in the back of a tractor trailer truck. By that time, he had actually begun speaking to me, and that day he told me something which caused me to experience a caterpillar-butterfly with him. He told me that the greatest days of his life had been when he was in the military, and that all his experience since that time had been miserable. He longed to return to military life, but he was too old, and that soured him on everything. I asked him what made military life preferable to civilian life, and he responded with a statement I will never forget. He stated, "In the military, if you hate the guy you are working next to, you can get a transfer; in the civilian workplace, you have to keep working next to him."

WOW! Talk about a knockout punch. He could not have hit me harder if he had smashed me with two rights and an uppercut left (which I'm sure he wanted to do on more than one occasion). I have never been more "impressed" by negative satisfaction in my life. Here was a man whose entire satisfaction goal in life was to flee his present situation (and almost every other potential situation in a normal work environment). His dream centered around getting away from people, and becoming a "work hermit." Satisfaction could only be attained by escape.

So what satisfies you? Or better yet, is there something that has to happen in order for you to be satisfied? As you contemplate this issue, think about your response as a reflection of your own self-assessment. What can you learn about yourself as a result of determining what satisfies you? How does this fit in with the total picture of examining who you are?

So far, we have examined some penetrating ways of looking at ourselves to perceive who we really are. We have taken a snapshot of ourselves, completed a "This Is Me" inventory, scrutinized our Caterpillar-Butterfly, engaged in a Brag Session, peered into our Goal Setting, and queried what tends to satisfy us. These are but a few of many ways of getting in touch with yourself, understanding who you are, introspectively realizing the real you, honestly seeking genuine self-feedback. There is another measure of self-understanding which I would like to introduce, but because of its magnitude and power, I want to devote an entire chapter to it. It will reveal to us what our basic nature is like, in terms of our psychological make-up and our behavioral tendencies. Let's take some time to examine our temperament types.

CHAPTER 2

◆◆◆

AT LEAST I'M CONSISTENT

**"My one regret in life
is that I am not
someone else."
– Woody Allen**

Are you more of an introvert or an extravert? Do you tend to assimilate information through your five senses or through your intuition? Are you more logical in your decision-making, or more emotional? Do you prefer closure, or do you like to keep your options open? Interesting questions! The answers to these may tell you more about yourself than you ever wanted to know. But a detailed self-examination of your temperament and tendencies is one of the most effective ways of understanding who you really are, and a necessary pre-requisite to truly understanding other people, which is the theme of a later chapter.

Perhaps you are already familiar with the *Myers-Briggs Type Indicator®. In my opinion, this type indicator is the most accurate predictor of human tendencies and behavior I have ever seen. It allows you to examine yourself in terms of your temperament, preferences and tendencies. It assists you in understanding who you are, and why you think and behave the way you do. It helps you to recognize your patterns of action as they relate to your personal and natural style. As my minister succinctly states, "Temperament lets you know how God wired you up." What he means is that temperament is something you enter this world already possessing. You cannot buy it or steal it. In fact, you don't even inherit it. As the father of twins, I can assure you that the

*Myers-Briggs Type Indicator and MBTI are registered trademarks of
  Consulting Psychologists Press, Inc.

temperaments of my boys were (and are, almost 19 years later) extremely different, and detectable at a very early age. Temperament is not determined by environment, culture, or family history. It can be altered, of course, by events or circumstances, and especially by conscious choice, but the "tendency" (key word) begins at birth (or earlier, in my opinion), and remains relatively unfazed throughout life.

A word about temperament—we are not talking about horoscopes, alien infiltration, or "vibes." We are dealing with behavioral tendencies, preferences, and real-life choices among a menu of options. Why is it that some children are naturally aggressive, while others tend to be passive? Why are some overly-curious, while others appear to be indifferent? Why do some seem to be more sensitive to adults than others? Why do certain children seem to have a penchant for math and science, while others gravitate toward language and spelling?

Have you ever witnessed two children attempting to accomplish a task that appears too difficult? One will give up and turn to another activity. The other will attack the problem, often tenaciously, and be satisfied only when he or she successfully completes the challenge. This is not a coincidence. The two children have different temperaments. They view their worlds in diverse ways. They make decisions based on various criteria. They are naturally-born different people. Just as there is diversity in nationalities, body types, genders (although only two that we know of), languages, hair and eye color, abilities, and cultures, there is a wide disparity in temperament types. We have artists and artisans. We have people who love to be in the limelight and people who dread being in groups of more than two. We have people who need to accumulate many friends and people who do not necessarily need other people to invigorate them. We have people who trust their "gut-reactions" almost exclusively and people who need to have concrete facts to support even minor decisions. We have people who prefer to discuss an item at least ten times before acting on it and people who cannot stand to leave a meeting without a final decision. These are temperament differences.

Please do not confuse temperament with behavior. Please do not confuse tendency with ability. We all have the ability to change our behavior to accommodate the task at hand, or to accomplish what is needed for success. But our tendencies remain the same (hence the word "tendency"). Let me give you an example. On a piece of scratch paper, sign your name as if you were giving an autograph or writing a check.

Pretty simple, wasn't it (unless the check was to the IRS)? Now, put your pen in the other hand, and sign your name again. Let's do question and answer.

Q: Could you do it?
A: Probably so.

Q: Was it comfortable?
A: Probably not.

Q: Was the second signing as natural as the first one?
A: Probably not.

Q: If you did it over and over again for many days, months, and years, would you get pretty good at it?
A: Probably so.

Q: Would it ever become as natural as the hand you were used to using before you tried the experiment?
A: Probably not.

This is what temperament is all about. It is the natural tendency you possess to think about, feel about, act on, and react to the events and situations in life.

Let me briefly walk you through four temperament differences. Please remember that these are tendencies only (we have the ability to perform in many different ways), and that these are not either-or tendencies, but rather they are "more likely than, less likely than" tendencies. For example, if you were to ask me if I am a man or a woman, I would state with considerable certainty that I am a man. But if you were to ask me if a am a classical music person or a popular music person, I would not be able to answer so definitively. I guess I tend to be more of a popular music fan (especially if it emanates from the 60s), but I also enjoy classical music, and there are times when I much prefer it over popular music. So what does that tell you about me? It says that I typically have a preference, but it is not set in concrete, nor is it true all the time. It can fluctuate, depending on the circumstances or my own mood. It does not box me in to being a uni-dimensional person, but it does tell me something about myself in terms of how I tend to appreciate music.

So, what are these temperament differences, and how do they identify who I am? How do they assist me in understanding who I am, so that I can grasp my own identity, and truly appreciate other people in a new light?

EXTRAVERT – INTROVERT

The most succinct way to describe an extravert (in many dictionaries, the preferred spelling is *extrovert*; however, in almost all temperament type literature, the spelling is *extravert*) is to say that the person becomes energized by being around other people. This person hardly ever tires of socialization. Attending a party is an uplifting experience, but is made even more euphoric by the knowledge that another party will begin when the present one ends. The extravert is outer-directed, scheduling much of life around interactions with other people. He or she craves group interaction, and exhibits a tireless stamina when dealing with others.

The introvert is one who becomes emotionally drained after too much social stimulation, and requires time alone to re-group, re-tool, and re-energize. The introvert tends to be inner-directed, gaining energy from time alone, or with a few select others. He or she can give the appearance of being extraverted (numerous comedians and other performers are introverts in "real life"), but this person requires quiet time and intimacy with self to prepare for the next group encounter. Two examples should help illustrate this difference.

> *Extravert—I could party all night.*
> *Introvert—Enough already. Get me out of here.*

In a former life, I was a consultant to colleges and universities, assisting them in developing and implementing adult education programs. In this capacity, I traveled a great deal, working with numerous people on their campuses. I am a strong extravert, and my partner at that time was an introvert. She enjoyed the work, and was extremely good at it. But the non-stop nature of our activities had different effects on us. One day, we consulted with a college in Ohio. Early that morning, we flew out of Chicago-O'Hare airport, landed in Detroit, rented a car, and drove to the college. For the next six or seven hours, we met with various groups, explaining the program concept and answering numerous questions from dozens of people. We were "on stage" the entire day. Both of us maintained a high energy level the whole time, and no one would have known which of us was extraverted and which one was introverted.

As we piled into our rental car for the return trip to the airport, we simultaneously revealed our temperament types, which caused both of us to laugh uproariously. Cindy settled into the passenger seat, demanding solitude and opportunity for sleep. I leaped into the driver's side of the car, boldly announcing that I hoped the plane ride was long enough for me to record all my notes from the day's meetings. Do you see what the experience did to us, based on our temperaments? Cindy, who was magnificent during the meetings, was drained by the interaction, and needed to re-group and return to her normal personhood. I was so energized by the interaction that I couldn't wait to do more work. The activities which drained Cindy actually "zoomed" me, and I needed further activity as a result. Incidentally, there are many times when I think Cindy is a whole lot smarter than I am, and will outlive me by 30 years.

A second example of a different nature: one of my twin boys is an extreme extravert (he even had to be <u>born</u> with another baby present), while the other is a moderate introvert/extravert. One day when they were about eight years old, they were playing outside with about five or six of their friends. From time to time I watched their activities and, at one point, noticed that while Matthew was still playing with their friends, Michael had retreated to the position of riding his bike alone. Not being sensitive to differences in temperament types and their importance, I quickly and ignorantly assumed that Michael had been ostracized by the others, mocked, embarrassed, and driven to exclusion. After all, they were together, and he was alone. To an extravert like me, that signaled trouble. I quickly changed into my Superman outfit, and charged to the rescue. I intercepted Michael's ride, and begged him to tell me what the other kids had done to him to cause him to depart the group activity. He calmly informed me that no one had hurt him, embarrassed him, mocked him, or wounded him. He just decided to ride his bike for a while.

Excuse me! What normal child chooses to be alone while there are other kids on the planet? I learned a solid lesson that day, which I have re-lived hundreds of times since. While I will never be introverted, I have gained understanding of those who are, and learned to appreciate their need for solitude and reflection.

We could go on and on for hours about extraverts and introverts, but this is meant to be merely an introduction to type, to assist us in understanding who we are. Besides, I have been here at the computer long enough. I need to go find a party with lots of people.

So which do you tend to be—an E (extravert) or an I (introvert)? Having this knowledge is helpful in self-examination.

SENSOR – INTUITOR

This temperament pair is the only one of the four which deals with how we assimilate information from our environments—the other three deal with how we "do" life (think, act, etc). This pair is about receiving data and stimuli, and sorting it out.

The sensor is someone who uses his or her five senses to interpret information, while the intuitor uses hunches or intuition to interpret the same information. Have you heard the expression, "You can't see the forest for the trees?" That is a description of a sensor, who tends to count trees, while an intuitor visualizes the entire forest. The sensor tends to focus on tangible things, while the intuitor tends to focus on intangible things. Sensors are more realistic, while intuitors are more idealistic. Sensors make excellent managers (they are practical and they get things done), while intuitors make excellent leaders (they are not always practical, but they tend to have dreams and vision). I am a strong sensor, and a few years ago I worked with a man who is a strong intuitor. One day he said to me, "I am good at getting the balloon up in the air." I responded, "Yes, and I am good at making sure it has air in it first." See the difference in those styles?

Sensor—I'll spell it out for you.
Intuitor—I can see it in your eyes.

Sensors are prone to limiting their options (they play within the rules), while intuitors sometimes ignore the rules in order to maximize their opportunities. It often takes a good intuitor to come up with an earth-shattering idea, but he or she usually needs a good sensor to make the idea a reality. In order to be effective, it is good to have both types.

School Daze

Monica was an excellent student in both grade school and high school. Her grades were straight As and Bs, and she never really struggled with academics. In addition, she scored high on the ACT and the SAT. During her first year of college, however, Monica suffered some severe setbacks. Even though she studied a great deal more than in high school, she did not do as well. She received two Cs, four Bs, and an A, but even worse, she found herself not enjoying school as she once had. Her courses seemed to be difficult for her, and she had trouble grasping what appeared to be important to the professors. This was puzzling to her, since she took fewer courses than in high school, and had less social involvement. Her parents attributed the change to such things as living away from home, having to be more self-responsible, being isolated from many of her former friends, etc.

While some of these things were probably legitimate factors, there may well have been another significant element—her temperament type. Monica was a strong sensor, and elementary and secondary education rewards sensors by teaching to their preferred learning styles. Most teachers of K-12 grades are sensors, and most curricula are "sensor-oriented." That is to say, they require sensor thinking—names, dates, events, one-right-answer, memorization, quizzes that are true-false or multiple choice. There is little room in K-12 grades for exploration, imagination, theory-building, or conceptualization. Sensor-type students have the advantage until age 18.

But something happens at the college level. Research indicates that most instructors and professors tend to be intuitors, and they teach that way. They look for concepts, trends, and relationships. They are not as concerned with the date of a certain event, or where it took place, but rather with how catastrophic it was in terms of national or world impact, what precedents it set, how it affected the global economy, etc. Intuitive teachers like to play with ideas, and the really effective ones are good at getting students to imagine instead of memorize, to think divergently rather than convergently.

So what happened to Monica? She tried to "do" college the same way she "did" high school, with less than excellent results. She struggled because she had to step outside her preferred style of being a sensor, and she had to become a quasi-intuitor. She could no longer do well by memorizing or forming acronyms as study aids (did you learn how to spell "arithmetic" by repeating, <u>A</u> <u>R</u>at <u>I</u>n <u>T</u>he <u>H</u>ouse <u>M</u>ay <u>E</u>at <u>T</u>he <u>I</u>ce <u>C</u>ream)? Try doing that with quantum physics or the theory of relativity.

I can personally identify with Monica's struggles. In college, I was a history major, mainly because I had done so well at it in high school, and I found it fascinating (great idea in high school—terrible idea in college). I have a better-than-average memory, and it served me well grade-wise in high school. I shared Henry Ford's definition of history. He posited, "History is nothing more than the succession of one damn thing after another." But when I went to college, history took on a whole new unpleasant meaning. I distinctly remember sitting in a class, and hearing the professor state, "Today I want to cover three main points." I instantly pulled out three sheets of paper and labeled them 1, 2, 3. Fifty minutes later, I was still uncertain what the three points had been. Other students exited the room, commenting on how fascinating the lecture had been, and how they had been enlightened on the subject. I grabbed them one-by-one, asking, "What were his three main points? I didn't get them, and they will probably be on the next test." So the Intuitor walked away with knowledge and satisfaction, while I walked away with an ever-growing ulcer.

Sensors and intuitors receive data in different manners. Sensors are designated by the letter "S" and intuitors by the letter "N" (since the letter "I" has already been used to identify Introverts). In fact, sometimes you will see "iNtuitor."

So which is more characteristic of you, sensing or intuiting? To understand this is to add another piece to the puzzle of knowing who you are.

THINKER – FEELER

Have you ever had anyone call you cold, hard, cruel, and heartless? On the other hand, have you ever had anyone call you blubbering, soft, a bleeding heart liberal, wearing your heart on your sleeve? If so, you already know something about the thinker and the feeler, but only from the opposition viewpoint, in an effort to criticize you for the way you are. Let's take a closer look at what these terms mean for self-examination and appreciation.

The thinker is one who uses logic and rationality in order to form opinions and make decisions. He or she usually becomes personally detached from the decision-making process, and is able to view it from the position of an outsider, even if it is an emotional issue. The thinker is objective, and will usually not allow his or her own personal feelings or emotions to get in the way of deciding. This person may elect a path that is not necessarily to his or her liking, but choose it because it makes sense, or is the logical thing to do.

The feeler is one who uses emotions and personal feelings in order to form opinions and make decisions. He or she usually becomes personally involved in the decision-making process, and has difficulty viewing it as an outsider. The more emotional the issue, the more personally involved and opinionated the feeler will become. In fact, even an issue which appears to be totally non-emotional to the thinker may be extremely heart-felt to the feeler. This person involves his or her own personal feelings and emotions when deciding or forming an opinion, and will typically choose the path which is to his or her liking, regardless of the logic or illogic of the decision.

Thinker—Facts don't lie.
Feeler—I don't want to believe it.

Because of my background and interests, I tend to use sports analogies to illustrate life and learning concepts. I realize that some of you reading this book actually are aware of activities other than sports which go on in this world. So allow me to use a sports analogy here, and then follow it with another illustration which is not related to athletics.

Two friends (one a thinker and the other a feeler) are avid Chicago Bears fans. On a particular Sunday in November, the Green Bay Packers are playing the Detroit Lions, and it would be to the Bears' advantage for the Packers to win the game, as the Lions and Bears are tied for first place. The thinker roots vigorously for the Packers (the hated Packers) so that the Bears will gain the advantage over the Lions. The feeler cannot bring himself to root for the Packers under any circumstances. The thinker uses logic in an attempt to convince his friend that it is best for the Bears if the Packers win. To the thinker, it is a "no-brainer." To root for the Lions is to root against the Bears—it just makes sense.

Why can't this idiot understand that? The feeler, on the other hand, understands the logic perfectly, but cannot in good conscience cheer for the Packers, as that would involve an act of treason against the Bears. The feeler knows that on Judgment Day, he will be held accountable for rooting for the Packers. Do you understand where these two friends are coming from? One uses logic as a basis for decision-making, while the other uses emotions.

For those who prefer movies to athletics, picture yourself (no pun intended) as a feeler selecting a movie to watch with your thinker spouse or friend. You are in the mood for a love story while he or she would prefer a historical movie or an intense whodunit. You extol the virtues of kicking back and relaxing in the warm glow of relationship and togetherness, but your partner argues that his or her choice is more beneficial in that you can both learn something from the historical movie that you did not know before. You try to explain that the purpose of this activity is for the two of you to be together and have a fun night, but he or she views it as a time-waster unless some practical and useful knowledge can be gained. To you, the activity is personal and is meant to focus on your relationship, while to him or her the activity itself must have meaning, producing the best of both worlds—relationship and learning. Do you see how the different desires emanate from diverse temperaments? Logic and emotions conflict in the decision-making process.

It is common to assume that thinkers are not emotionally sensitive people, that they have no "heart" whatsoever for children, grandmothers, and small dogs. That is not the case. Thinkers can be every bit as sensitive as feelers, sometimes even more so, but they tend to use their logical side when forming opinions or making decisions. They might not like the decision, but they determine they have to make it. They are quite concerned with concepts such as fairness, principles, standards, and justice. Feelers are mostly concerned with concepts such as values, personal opinion, loyalty, and humane behavior.

Another common assumption is that all feelers are compassionate and forgiving, while all thinkers are uncaring and unforgiving. Not so! Some of the most vicious people on earth are feelers. They just make decisions or form opinions subjectively instead of objectively. Let me illustrate how the different types might respond to a situation which occurs in their community.

You read in the newspaper that a lady stole a new-born baby from the hospital. After about five days, the baby is recovered—well-nourished, unharmed, and in perfect health. With no further information, what do you think should be done with the "kidnapper?"

Let's look at four possible responses, based on temperament type.

The <u>compassionate feeler</u> might desire leniency for the lady, pointing out the care she took for the baby while it was "hers." She is probably very lonely, and she may have even had her own child die in infancy. She obviously meant no harm to the baby. At worst, she should be accused of poor judgment, and punished accordingly. In fact, she should be afforded help for her emotional condition.

The <u>compassionate thinker</u> might desire leniency for the lady, stating that ultimately, no harm was done. If "an eye for an eye" is the rule, then she should be gently punished, and monitored so that she does not have opportunity to repeat her offense. Had she injured the child, even accidentally, she should receive maximum punishment. When you take a chance and go outside of the rules, you suffer the consequences. But because she did not injure the baby, then she should receive minimal punishment.

The <u>vindictive feeler</u> might desire maximum punishment for the lady, citing the terror and grief she caused for the mother. Even though she took good care of the baby (that was the very <u>least</u> of what she could do), she is responsible for the extreme anxiety she caused, and for what could have happened to the baby. How would she like it if someone did that to her? She should somehow be made to feel the mother's pain, to teach her a lesson. If she is a sick woman, then we should get her some help, but first she needs to be taught a lesson that you don't do that to other people.

The <u>vindictive thinker</u> might desire maximum punishment for the lady because she broke a serious law, and that cannot be allowed in a civilized society. If she is not punished, regardless of circumstances, it sets a dangerous precedent. It is true that she did no harm to the baby, but that is not the point. There is no right way to do a wrong thing, and her admirable care for the baby does not obliterate the fact that she stole it in the first place.

Here is a key concept to remember. Do you see how different types of people can arrive at the <u>same</u> decision-making conclusions, but from different perspectives? **The decisions you make do not reveal your temperament type styles (even to yourself). You need to investigate the reasons behind those decisions, and the motivations which elicited the responses.** So which do you identify with more, the thinker or the feeler? Are you more logical or emotional when it comes to making decisions or solving problems? This is another way of helping you to assess who you are.

JUDGER – PERCEIVER

This last temperament type pair deals with the concepts of closure and open-endedness. Try not to concentrate on the words judging and perceiving, as they may be confusing with regard to what this really means. A judger is not one who judges other people, and a perceiver is not one who perceives well (like an intuitor). A judger is one who seeks closure and finality. This person thrives on settling issues rather than leaving them "hanging" or open-ended. The judger is addicted to structure—meetings should begin and end on time, you should be where you are supposed to be, once a decision is made it is final, deadlines should be adhered to, decisiveness needs to be saluted, and planning ahead is next to godliness.

The perceiver basks in the glow of flexibility and choice. To a perceiver, nothing is ever set in cement. This person always keeps his or her options open. "There is always a better mousetrap" is a perceiver commandment. Why lock yourself into a decision when you may encounter evidence later which suggests a change in stance? Structure is inhibiting. Go with the flow whenever possible. Never say "never."

Of the four different elements in temperament, this may well be the most easy to identify. In fact, with many people, this is the area where their scores are most diverse. People tend to be either judgers or perceivers, with not much overlap. I have also noticed that some people who really are perceivers will score themselves as judgers, because their jobs require "judging" behavior, and they subsequently view themselves in that light. Upon further review, they often recognize their perceiving nature.

Judger—It's 11:57 a.m.
Perceiver—It's a little before noon.

Let me give you an example of typical behaviors of these two types. Picture a meeting set for 10:00 am. At 9:55, the judgers are seated in the meeting room, with notebooks open, coffee poured, agenda memorized, and a teleconference planned for 11:30, which is the posted end time for this meeting. Between 10:00 and 10:10, the perceivers file into the meeting room. Some have forgotten their notebooks, and retreat to their offices to retrieve them. Others have just made coffee, and need to wait for it to brew. Still others consult with colleagues to determine where they will go for lunch, and then they inquire what the agenda is for this meeting. Why are they here anyway?

Does any of this sound familiar? Judgers cannot handle the "laissez-faire" attitude of perceivers, and perceivers absolutely loathe the intractable stubbornness of judgers. Perceivers are labeled as indecisive, time-wasters, uncommitted, and wishy-washy. Judgers are labeled as impulsive, compulsive, obsessive, and inflexible (by the way, I have used only the most charitable of terms I have heard people utter when describing the opposite type).

When the actual meeting begins, the scenario gets worse. Judgers want to keep the agenda flowing, while perceivers could care less about the agenda (if indeed they even know what it is). Judgers want to take action on each item, while perceivers are content to table them until a later meeting. Judgers want to end the meeting at precisely 11:30, while perceivers desire to extend it to as long as people are able to meet, regardless of the time. Incidentally, if you are still uncertain as to whether you are a judger or a perceiver, here is a sure-fire test. You are on item number three of an eight-item agenda, and someone says, "Can we move to item number seven? I am really interested in that issue." What is your reaction?

A personal anecdote: I was in a meeting once where the faculty and I were to determine which two students would receive a scholarship, from a pool of six students. The discussion was lively and lengthy, the merits of each applicant were reviewed thoroughly, and eventually a decision was reached which was agreed to by each faculty member. After the issue was settled, and we were about to move to a different issue, one faculty member suggested, "Candidate C probably should also have been considered in the final vote." I commented to her, "Only a perceiver would make a statement like that after a long discussion and a unanimous vote had been taken." She didn't actually say anything, but if looks could kill . . .

To buy or not to buy—that is the question.

Let's look at a hypothetical scenario. A judger goes to a store to purchase a sweater. Typically, this person will know in advance what to buy—color, style, price. He or she buys the sweater, takes it home, and wears it. If it is not right, the judger might take it back to the store (for an exchange, not a refund), or give it away or let it sit in a drawer forever. The perceiver who purchases the sweater will take it home, then begin to question whether or not it should have been bought and what it will go with, and may decide to return it later. Here's the point—typically the judger will consider the transaction complete and final. He or she made the purchase (right or wrong), and will live with the consequences. The perceiver does not typically consider a transaction to be completed, and will leave options open.

The judger is classified with the letter J, while the perceiver is labeled with the letter P.

So where do you fit in? Are you a judger or a perceiver, or do you fit somewhere in the middle? Do you feel more comfortable with closure or open-endedness? Do you like structure or flexibility? Do you like things settled or tabled? Do you prefer to wrap it up, or to leave it open? Knowing what style you possess in this regard is another step toward knowing who you are as a person.

CHAPTER 3

◆◆◆

IF AT FIRST YOU DON'T SUCCEED . . .

"Anyone who doesn't make
mistakes isn't trying hard enough."
Lessons From Attila The Hun

I'm sure you have read the same stories I have—how Abraham Lincoln lost almost every election he entered until he became President in 1860, how the vast percentage of Thomas Edison's inventions were failures, how most of Leonardo DiVinci's creations never materialized, and how most admired and successful people in the business world today got there only after numerous attempts and repeated failures and rejections. Happily, it only takes one momentous victory to make us forget all about the past miseries and frustrations, and to motivate us to loftier and greater goals.

Why do so many people avidly play golf week after week, when 80% of their shots are unremarkable? Because in a typical round, they hit that one shot that Arnold Palmer and Tiger Woods would envy, and it keeps them coming back for more. Last summer, my sons and I played golf with one of my best friends, who is also a colleague. His game that day was hardly better than my own, which usually is a synonym for humiliation. But on the eighth hole, he lofted a shot 152 yards from the tee into the cup for a hole-in-one. He was ecstatic! We talked about it for weeks. He found a way to insert the story into several conversations during meetings. It was a brush with fame and immortality, and next April when the snow begins to melt, I expect a phone call from him asking me how quickly I can drive to the nearest golf course.

Try, try again.

If at first you don't succeed, try, try again. That suggestion was no doubt created by a judger, because a perceiver would have uttered, "If at first you don't succeed, try something different, or alter your expectations." But most of us have learned that perseverance does indeed typically pay off, and the dividends are more than rewarding. Precious few people have "skated" through life (with apologies to Peggy Fleming, Eric Heiden, and Bonnie Blair). Most of us have been humbled by our attempts at athletics, scholastics, oratory, and repairing a leaky faucet. We have learned that if we don't get back up on the horse, we will live with frustration, discontentment, mediocrity, and less than we bargained for. Someone once noted that success is 10% inspiration and 90% perspiration. While the percentages may not be exact, the point is well-taken (one has to be careful with percentages since Yogi Berra once explained that success in baseball is 90% pitching, and the other half is defense). Most of life seems to be recovery, and the most successful individuals are those who recover most effectively.

Before reading on, look back at the last paragraph from the previous chapter. The final couple of sentences indicate where we want to go right now. Before we can successfully move into the realm of understanding, accepting, and celebrating others, we need to accomplish two tasks. First, we want to be certain that our self-perceptions are accurate, and second, we want to be satisfied with who we are. In both cases, if we end up confused or dissatisfied, we need to try, try again. Otherwise, it will not work, and our efforts will be futile at best and misleading at worst. If I try to see others through a distorted vision, the image will be too blurry to be of any help. I need to be certain I have the proper prescription glasses, and they have to be clean. I may think I see a house kitten, but before I attempt to pet and feed it, I want to be sure it isn't a mountain lion—otherwise, the feeding will take care of itself.

There is a very real danger here, which we alluded to in Chapter One. If my self-perceptions are inaccurate (either by innocent error or by intentional design), then my warped view of others will seem to be right. I will be able to justify my stereotypes, insensitivities, and callousness. I will conclude, "Now I really know myself, and other people who are different from me are still jerks!" Let's take a look at the accuracy of our self-perceptions, and at our satisfaction level with who we are.

How can I be sure that my self-perceptions are really correct? How can I know that my view is not jaundiced by my own biases? How can I be certain that who I think I am I really am? The best way I know to respond to those questions is really very simple—ask other people. Find a cadre of five or six people who know you well and have them share their own perceptions with you. Explain to them that you are not looking for compliments, kudos, or affirmation. You are seeking honesty and assistance in your quest to discover the real you. Allow them to review the exercises you completed in Chapter One—the snapshot, "This Is Me," Caterpillar-Butterfly, your brag session, your goals, your satisfactions, and from Chapter Two, your temperament type. Ask them if they would agree with your responses.

What would they change? Add? Delete? How do they see you differently from how you see yourself? For the past several years, I have had my adult students complete the "This Is Me" exercise. It is amazing what they learn about themselves when receiving feedback from their classmates. For example, do you remember the sentence which read, "I like people who are. . .?" Some people write words like "honest, reliable, and loving" while others write "punctual, producers, and non-smokers." Do you see how different temperament types interpret sentences in diverse ways? Your friends might be able to lend some insight as to how you tend to view people and situations.

"The best mirror is an old friend."
– George Herbert
(quoted in <u>Familiar Quotations</u>, p. 324)

If you are really sincere (not to mention gutsy) about checking out your self-perceptions, ask some of your more trusted friends to share with you a few of the areas of your life which they think could be improved. For example, "Do I tend to be prejudicial, pushy, negative, presumptuous, haughty, insensitive, domineering, arrogant, manipulative, selfish, materialistic, pompous, or rude?" If they answer "yes" to all of the above, I would suggest that you have problems far beyond the scope of this book. In fact, I am shocked that you found five people who admit to being your friends. On the other hand, if they say, "No, but you don't sing very well, and your finger nails need trimming," then you have every right to consider yourself an OK person, and your self-perceptions may well be accurate. I worded this in a less-than-serious tone, but please don't dismiss the concept. You may not feel that you tend to be negative, or insensitive, or manipulative, but if several of your closest cronies suggest that you are, then an honest person will note those issues for further scrutiny. I once heard a speaker admonish, "If one person says you are a horse, ignore it; if two people say you are a horse, look in the mirror; if three people say you are a horse, buy a saddle." It may be only a matter of perception or a misunderstanding, or it may be the truth.

This is when things get touchy, because most of us tend to be rather fragile beings, and when our feelings get hurt or we feel attacked, our defenses rise to the occasion. Because our perceptions are different from those of others, when we receive feedback that is not consistent with what we believe to be true (which psychologists term "cognitive-dissonance"), we tend to react from an emotional perspective because we are perceiving a too-close-to-home and unwarranted siege. Let me provide you with a personal example.

I tend to have a "controlling" nature, although I prefer not to call it that. Because I have a tendency to think things out well in advance and be prepared for almost any emergency or snafu, I am perceived by some other people as being "controlling." I tend to be obnoxiously early to everything so that I will never be late (which to me is the apex of insult). I typically enter a meeting well-prepared, so that there can never be any surprises. I anticipate that other people, or nature itself, will throw me a curve ball along the way, and I attempt to anticipate it in advance, and be prepared for its eventuality. I believe strongly in contingency plans, in case the first one fails or is sabotaged. If someone is to be trusted with information, documents, or money, I suggest that it be me, because I have great confidence in my ability to produce and deliver when appropriate.

There are some people who interpret my attitudes and actions as being controlling, in a negative sense of the word. While I do not agree with that accusation, I can certainly <u>understand</u> why they feel that way. I do attempt to be in control in situations where I believe I am capable, although I quickly yield in situations where I feel others have more experience and opportunity for our mutual success. I have never attempted to suggest to a doctor how to perform a certain operation, or informed a pilot how to fly the aircraft. But people close to me have suggested from time to time that they feel left out of the information loop, that I make decisions without consulting with them first, that I assume things on my own without input from them, that I tend to be "controlling."

This is information that I did not receive from my self-perceptions, as I never saw myself in that light. It had to be garnered from feedback through discussions with others close to me. It is information that had to be filtered to me outside of my own tunnel vision. While I did not want to acknowledge it or accept it, it could only be acquired from sources which are far more objective than I could ever be.

So what are my options? How can I deal with this problem? Actually, I have several different alternatives. First, I can ignore it. I can state that it is a problem only to others, not to me. Since I am aware of my positive intentions, I can dismiss the misperceptions of others, and continue to perform as I always have. Case closed!

Second, I can explain to the friends what my motives are. I can tell them that it is my nature to be in control, that I am very good at being the captain, that I rarely make mistakes, that they are wise to trust me, and that they will probably thank me in the long run because they will benefit from my handling of the situation. They should assume my good intentions, and they should realize that they will be better off because of my aggressive stance. The "C" word (control) is not necessarily bad.

Third, I can misinterpret their motives for confronting me. I can (through tunnel vision) not understand or respect their views. I can (ignorantly) assume they are idiots who do not understand leadership potential when they see it. I can perceive them as jealous of my take-charge-style, envious of my ability to take the bull by the horns. Because of my inaccurate self-perceptions, I can assume that my style is "right," therefore, every other style is wrong. I can arrogantly (and this can be an uninformed or benign arrogance) dismiss their views as absurd because they are not in concert with my own. If they had brains, they would be dangerous. Why can't they be normal like me?

Fourth, I can hear out the comments and criticisms, weigh their validity, and determine how to respond. Here I need to ask a crucial question. Which is more important to me—the issue or the relationship? If the issue is most critical, I will probably resort to my "controlling" style. I will assume command, and attempt to make the "right" decision for all involved. Feelings can be patched up later, along with amends. But if the relationship is most important, then I need to adjust my style. I need to let go of the control issue, to not be as concerned with the outcome of the problem as with the outgrowth of the relationship. I may need to sacrifice the product for the process.

Pretend you are me for a moment (I once asked someone what he would do if he were in my shoes, and he replied, "I would shine them"). My boss has asked me to make a decision which will affect my entire department. Because of my past experience in the job, and the fact that I am privy to some information which others in the department do not have, I instinctively have a good idea which decision would be most beneficial for all concerned. I also know that if I put it to a general vote, the result may not come out the way I think it should. If I seek the opinions of others, then they will know that I am in this quandary, and they will suggest that we all discuss the issue and vote on the decision. If I isolate a few trusted colleagues for their input, and others discover my covert solicitation, then I am being exclusionary in their eyes, and I have even bigger problems. If I just make the decision myself, then I am back to being "controlling." So what am I to do? Other than applying polish to my shoes, what would you do if you were wearing them?

Let's go back two paragraphs. I stated that if the issue itself is the most critical element in the decision-making, then I would probably resort to my natural style, and live with the consequences of being labeled "controlling." Or I might seek input from others, but expend a great deal of energy convincing them that my opinion is the best one for our department. However, if the issue is not as critical to me as is the relationship I have with my co-workers and staff, and if I surmise that they view me as a controlling person, then I will seek input from everyone possible, and encourage the group to arrive at a decision which we all can support (the advantage here is that if it turns out to be a wrong decision, I have people I can blame it on). Some people believe that the ultimate quality of a successful leader is the ability to take credit for all the outstanding decisions, and find others to blame for the bad ones.

I wanted to provide this example in order to illustrate how one might act in response to a situation which involves control, but now let's return to the broader issue of the accuracy of our self-perceptions. I suggested that soliciting input from trusted friends and colleagues is a wonderful way to assess the accuracy of self-perceptions. There are two reasons for this. First, good friends have the ability to point out flaws, discrepancies, and inconsistencies with tact and love. They want to speak the truth, while vigorously avoiding hurting your ego. They recognize your quest to become a better person, and they attempt to assist you in that endeavor, all the while supporting you and trying not to damage your self-esteem. This is the by-product of having built a healthy relationship between you. We will devote an entire chapter of this book to that concept, as it is absolutely crucial for successful interactions with others. The second reason why we should seek assistance from friends in order to gauge our self-perceptions is equally obvious—they can be more objective in their assessment of us, they do not possess the same tunnel vision regarding us that we have, and they usually have a broader perspective than we do in terms of how we come across to others. Let me provide an example of this.

I once worked with a man who had a terribly chauvinistic reputation with the women where we worked. Virtually every woman who had contact with him at the office literally hated him for his sexism. In today's world, he would have spent every penny he owned and the vast majority of his time fighting off charges of sexual harassment. The man could hardly open his mouth without offending someone. But here is the kicker—he had no idea that he was obnoxious, offensive, or invasive. He was not aware that his comments were un-welcomed, or that his attempts at humor were inappropriate. In his mind he was innocent, witty, friendly, and appreciated.

He once said to one of our female co-workers, "You look very nice today. You must be going to a meeting or something." On another occasion, he commented on a proposal written by another female co-worker by stating, "This is extremely well-written. Your husband must have helped you with it." These are but two of numerous similar remarks he made. Notice how in each case he would have been OK if he had stopped after the first sentence ("You look very nice today." "This is extremely well-written"). It was the follow-up sentence that got him in trouble every time. But he was not aware that he came across to people as a sexist. Had he confided in a trusted friend that he was in search of continuous improvement in his life, and had he sought assistance in revealing possible flaws or inappropriate behaviors, that would have served him well in terms of his reputation and relationships.

There is another element to this scenario that should be considered. I mentioned earlier that it is a gutsy move to ask trusted friends to share with you a few of the areas of your life which they think could be improved. I emphasize that you should do this only if you are willing to listen, seriously consider their comments and criticisms, and be willing to make some life adjustments if they are warranted. Otherwise, your interaction with your friends is a total sham, and they will know it. They will realize that your inclusion of their opinions was a manipulative effort to affirm your status quo, and it could very possibly throw some darts into your relationship. I am not suggesting that you immediately "buy into" every comment made, or create a twelve-step program for yourself because someone mentioned that you occasionally interrupt others while they are talking, but I am strongly encouraging honest introspection, which includes active listening, honest questioning and scrutiny, and willingness to admit that maybe some change in your attitudes and behavior might be advantageous.

Before we move on, and hopefully without belaboring the point into oblivion, let me emphasize one more time how critical it is that we listen to our friends with an open mind and a non-defensive attitude. If we are going to argue with their perceptions or dismiss their evaluations as misunderstandings of us, then we need to vacate the charade, and abandon the pretense of better understanding ourselves. At that point, we should conclude that everyone else is out-of-step and misguided. We should protect our egos by assuming that they are either uninformed, jealous or downright vicious. Above all, we should quit reading this book, because the rest of it is based on a serious and healthy understanding of self, and a committed and determined desire to appreciate others, and interact with them in the most positive manner possible.

Let's look at a hypothetical interchange. You have requested that a trusted friend apprise you of an area of your social life which he or she thinks could be improved. The friend says to you, "You tend to interrupt people in the middle of their sentences in order to counter their statements or interject your own opinions." This is shocking news to you, as you are unaware that you do this. In fact, you are convinced that you do <u>not</u> do this. What options do you have in responding to your friend, other than the most obvious one, which is to interrupt him or her in mid-sentence to deny the allegation?

1. "Wrong, I don't do that."
2. "Everyone does that from time to time."
3. "If I don't speak up, I will never be heard."
4. "I am unaware that I do that, but I will try to be aware of it in my discussions during the next few days."
5. "I will ask three or four more trusted friends if they also think I have that tendency."

The first response is denial. The second and third are justifications. The last two are representative of someone who is honestly seeking self-improvement. Notice there does not have to be guilt, shame, embarrassment, or loss of self-esteem associated with this introspection. If there is a problem, let's identify it, confirm it, and work on resolving it. (I must confess here that because I am a thinker, it is easy for me to say and do that. Feelers have a more difficult time being objective about such "self-issues" because they tend to internalize the scrutiny. Thinkers need to be sensitive to feelers in this regard.)

If you are serious about discovering areas of your life which are not obvious to you, but which may be screamingly apparent to your friends, there is a mechanism which you might consider. Have you ever heard of the Johari Window?* It was developed by two psychologists, Joseph Luft and Harry Ingham, and they named it after their first names, Joe and Harry. It is a model which centers around the concept of feedback, and one of its chief purposes is to allow people to see themselves as others see them. I won't elaborate too much at this point, as you can read about the Johari Window in depth in most communication textbooks, but look at the window below, with its four "panes."

PUBLIC	**BLIND**
PRIVATE	**UNKNOWN**

*From *Group Processes: An Introduction to Group Dynamics, Third Edition* by Joseph Luft. Copyright ©1984 by Joseph Luft. Reprinted by permission of Mayfield Publishing Company.

The "Public" area is that which is known to both you and others. It is what you are aware of and have chosen to share, or it is obvious, such as the color of your hair. The "Blind" area is that which is apparent to others, but not to you, such as the fact that you jingle the change in your pocket whenever you get nervous. The "Private" area is that which is known to you, but not to others. It is what you have chosen not to share, your deep, dark secrets, such as your craving for spumonti ice cream at midnight. The "Unknown" area is that which is hidden from everyone, including yourself. It might be labeled your subconscious.

For our purposes, concentrate on your "Blind" area. Ask your trusted friends to share with you their perceptions of your attitudes, strengths, weaknesses, behaviors, etc. Inquire of them what is healthy and unhealthy about you. Seek honest feedback in an attempt to strengthen your positives and reduce your negatives. In other words, widen your tunnel vision so as to incorporate more data in your search for true and realistic self-understanding.

I mentioned at the outset of this chapter that we are attempting to accomplish two tasks—being certain that our self-perceptions are accurate, and being satisfied with who we are. Assuming that we have conquered the first task to a greater or lesser degree (and recognizing that it will never be a "done deal" because it is an on-going struggle), let's turn our attention to the second task.

"My life needs editing."
– Mort Sahl

I recently had one of my adult students (who I will call Maggie) tell me how much she resented completing the temperament inventory because it only reinforced to her what she already knew about herself—that she was a <u>bad</u> person, and probably would never change. I tried to explain to her that we are not talking in terms of good or bad; we are talking about our tendencies, which are natural and in-born. Our actions and behavior may be good or bad, depending on any number of factors and expectations, but our tendencies should not cause us consternation or frustration. They only serve to identify our preferences, like whether we typically choose vanilla or chocolate ice cream. Maggie lamented that her temperament type suggested that she tends to be a "rescuer" (enabler is the more current buzzword), and that because of that tendency, she had become involved in a number of unhealthy relationships over the years. She resented (actually loathed) that trait, despised that segment of herself, and tried desperately to hide it in order to dismiss the pain. By completing the inventory, she was once again reminded of her tendency, and it caused great discomfort for her.

I told Maggie that before we can make alterations in our lives, we must first understand what needs to be changed or repaired. If I don't feel well, and suspect that there may be a significant physical malady, I don't rush to the pharmacy and load up on dozens of different drugs, hoping to cover all the bases. I also don't ignore the discomfort or pain, figuring it will pass with time. Instead, I make an appointment with my physician in an attempt to diagnose what the specific ailment might be, so as to treat it properly. Further, I don't despise the physical exam because it tells me something I don't want to hear. On the contrary, I welcome the opportunity to identify the area to be repaired. I may not like the news, but I embrace the journalist for revealing the part which needs attention.

I further delineated for Maggie the difference between a tendency and a behavior. I explained that she may have a tendency toward being a "rescuer," but that she did not have to follow through on that tendency with her behavior. She should not resent being knowledgeable about her preference, but rather be ecstatic that she has such insight, so that she is capable of making mature and healthy decisions. She said something like, "I always seem to fall into the same trap." I encouraged her that such recognition is a marvelous sign because it revealed her inclination, and gave her the opportunity to alter her behavior so as not to once again become a victim. Stated in simple terms—we may never change our tendencies and preferences, but we can utilize the knowledge they afford in order to behave in ways that will provide satisfaction with who we are. The flip side of such introspection is that it allows us to appreciate the positive attributes we have, and provides the motivation for strengthening those traits.

The question at this point seems to be, "Now that you have peered into several mirrors, do you like what you see?" Actually, this is not so much a yes or no question as it is a matter of degree. If I manage a kids' baseball team, which I often do, and someone asks me after a game, "Are you satisfied with how the game turned out?" I may not be able to respond in one syllable. If we won, I may suggest that I was pleased with the final score and with the offense, but that our pitching and base-running were less than spectacular, and will require attention if we are to compete for the championship. The same is true for our introspection. We may be quite satisfied with certain areas of our personalities, attitudes, and behaviors, but at the same time be concerned with our need for improvement in certain respects.

The purpose of this book is to provide measures of understanding ourselves, understanding others, and understanding how we can better communicate with and get along with those who are part of our lives, both personally and professionally. If you are 100% satisfied with who you are and how you interact with others in your life-space, then I would suggest you stop reading this book, and give it to someone else who probably needs it a lot more than you do. On the other hand, if you still observe areas where you could use improvement in truly knowing yourself, as I do constantly, and if you are still seeking ways to more effectively accept, appreciate, and communicate with others, then read on. Hopefully, something that is written here will push the right button or turn on a light bulb that will assist you in improving some aspect of your life. As a president of a company once shared with me, "If I get one good idea out of a speech or a book, it was well worth the time and effort." I trust what you read in this book will provide at least one insight which will significantly impact your life in a positive manner.

SUMMARY OF PART 1

The chief objective of Part 1 of this book has been to allow all of us the opportunity to get to know ourselves better. We have investigated the reasons for why it is advantageous to understand ourselves, and we have scrutinized a number of methods of self-evaluation. We have taken snapshots of ourselves, to ascertain what we look like, both physically and psychologically. We have completed a "This Is Me" inventory, to recognize our attitudes, desires, potentials, and perceptions. We have examined our growth from Caterpillar to Butterfly, to see how we have matured in our world views. We have bragged about our accomplishments and abilities, in order to recognize our on-going strengths and capabilities. We have set goals, to help us assess what we value and to motivate us toward further accomplishments. We have investigated what satisfies us, to realize how much control we have over our happiness. We have scrutinized our temperament types, to discover how we are wired up, and to recognize our tendencies and preferences. We have reexamined ourselves in terms of the accuracy of our self-perceptions, as well as the satisfaction level of where we are. We have discovered methods of eliminating our tunnel vision, so as to gain a more realistic picture of who we are. All in all, we have invested considerable time and effort in an attempt to discover the "real me," and to truly know ourselves.

Hopefully, this has been abundantly helpful in the quest for self-examination and understanding. If not, we need to return to other methods, because if we do not truly understand ourselves, we can never hope to understand others. If these chapters have been enlightening and illuminating, then we can proceed with the far more arduous and challenging task of understanding others, accepting and celebrating their differences, and improving ourselves in the process. If we honestly know ourselves, as The Oracle admonished, then we are ready for the Herculean task of understanding, accepting, and celebrating others. This is a difficult challenge, but one with potential rewards far above what we can imagine. In my opinion, nothing in this world can supplant a healthy, meaningful, and satisfying relationship, whether it be with a relative, lover, friend, co-worker, or acquaintance. Are you ready for the challenge?

PART 2

CHAPTER 4

◆◆◆

WHY CAN'T YOU BE PERFECT LIKE ME?

> **"A perfectionist is one who takes great pains—and gives them to other people."**
> ***Education Digest***
> **(quoted in *Quote Unquote*, p. 234)**

In Part 2 of this book, I would like for us to shift the focus away from "ME" and place it on "YOU." The YOU that I have in mind may be different from the YOU that you have in mind. YOUs are special people in our lives. They may be spouses or significant others, they may be sisters or brothers or other relatives, they may be bosses or co-workers, they may be special friends, or they may just be people who we deal with on a daily basis. They are not strangers and they are not enemies. YOUs are people who we love or like, admire and respect, feel close to and have a special affinity for; but YOUs are people who are different from us to a greater or lesser degree, and therefore we consider them imperfect. YOUs have tendencies we don't understand, styles we don't share, habits we don't emulate, partialities we don't appreciate, temperaments we don't imitate, and behaviors we don't readily accept. YOUs are people we get along with famously for the most part, but who drive us crazy from time to time because their ideas and actions are occasionally very weird.

YOUs are people we get along with famously for the most part, but who drive us crazy from time to time because their ideas and actions are occasionally very weird.

• For romantic Introverts, YOUs are people who would like to invite six other people over on your "date night."

• For party Extraverts, YOUs are people who want to watch the Super Bowl with just the two of you.

• For concrete Sensors, YOUs are people who ask you to imagine what your lives will be like ten years from now.

• For abstract Intuitors, YOUs are people who question your investment decision, based on the profit and loss statement.

• For sensitive Feelers, YOUs are people who insist on playing it by the book, regardless of the extenuating circumstances.

• For calculating Thinkers, YOUs are people who want the accused condemned or acquitted before the trial begins.

• For hungry Judgers, YOUs are people who insist on examining all 32 flavors before deciding which ice cream cone to order.

• For discriminating Perceivers, YOUs are people who ask you which movie you would have chosen had they not already purchased the tickets to the one they wanted to see.

In other words, YOUs, for all their lovable characteristics, don't quite measure up. They are good, but not great. They are great, but not magnificent. They are magnificent, but not perfect. They have flaws, and that is darned irritating! Why can't they be perfect like me?

Let me emphasize again—YOUs are not people we can dismiss. They are folks who are integral parts of our lives, and significant to us in a most positive way. We are talking about Adam and Eve (although it is rumored that Eve once asked Adam if he were seeing another woman), Romeo and Juliet, Rogers and Hammerstein, Sinatra and Martin, fire and rain, salt and pepper, Notre Dame and football, Beavis and Butthead, and most memorable of all, Fred and Ginger.

If YOUs were people we pass in the street, or stand with at the bus stop, or sit next to at a concert, this would not be so difficult. If YOUs were transparent people who we would not miss if they were to vanish from the earth, then this chapter would not be necessary. But because YOUs are people we care about, work with, confide in, make love with, sacrifice for, and need in our lives, the question which is the title of the chapter remains a crucial one. We all ask it from time to time, subconsciously if not overtly. No matter who the person is, no matter how close the relationship gets, once in a while we all scream out, "WHAT IS WRONG WITH YOU? HOW CAN YOU NOT SEE MY POINT? WHY MUST YOU BE SO DIFFICULT? WHY CAN'T YOU UNDERSTAND WHAT I AM SAYING? WHY CAN'T YOU BE PERFECT LIKE ME?"

A number of years ago when I was consulting with a university, one of the Vice-Presidents explained to me how he dealt with faculty members during conflict situations. These people were all YOUs in his life. He liked them, and he respected them, and yet he was fond of using the expression, "I negotiated them out of their argument." In other words, because he maintained status above them (Vice-President to faculty), he used his clout to make them see things his way, but he made it appear as though they were working toward mutual benefit, and so he referred to it as negotiating.

I have limited knowledge and experience in negotiation techniques, but I have considerable knowledge and experience in psychology and working with people, and I am quite confident that the approach suggested by that Vice-President of working out a disagreement or a confrontation situation will not lead to true resolution nor continued relationship symmetry. There is something about a vertical bias that prevents horizontal harmony. That is not a profound observation, but unfortunately it is the root cause of many a snafu in resolving pesky problems at the workplace. A supervisor and a supervisee have conflicting opinions on how best to solve a problem or improve a procedure. All too often, the supervisor pulls rank, refuses to consider the opposing argument, assumes that he or she has greater knowledge, implements his or her own idea, and calls it "negotiating." Why can't that darned employee be perfect like me?

Vertical bias prevents horizontal harmony.

I wish I had been the person who first coined the expression, "tunnel vision," because I really like it. I have been in many tunnels (both physical and mental), and it is true that there is only one perspective when your peripheral vision is non-existent. Since I live in Chicago, I ride the subway from time to time (I have also been on several in London, but those folks like to call it The Tube). When I am in the subway, with no daylight available, and with tracks that flow only north and south, I experience true tunnel vision. If I need to go from 300 West Division Street to 200 East Jackson Boulevard, I travel straight south to Jackson, then east to Michigan Avenue. If I were driving or walking, I could use any number of routes to arrive at my destination. I could zigzag one block at a time if I wanted to. But the subway limits my options, and it forces me to suffer from tunnel vision.

"Pride is the only disease known to man that makes everyone sick except the one who has it."
– Buddy Robinson
(quoted in Quote Unquote, p. 255)

The question, Why can't you be perfect like me?, is given birth because of tunnel vision. If I know of no approach other than my own, if I do not consider alternative opinions, if it is my way or the highway, then I must naively assume that my way is right, and any other way is wrong. I am perfect, and if you are not on my track, then you are imperfect. Jean Piaget was a Swiss educator, and he popularized the concept of egocentrism. **This is the inability of someone to see things from any perspective other than his or her own.** Perception becomes reality. In other words, what one "sees" and therefore assumes to be true is actually true in his or her mind. Any contradictory evidence must be wrong or tainted because the person's "reality" is already set in cement. We expect to see this in young children, due to their lack of experience and maturity, but it is exceedingly distressing when it appears in individuals who are chronologically mature. Let me provide an example for you.

During the time when I was preparing college students for a career in teaching, I visited one of my student teachers in a first grade classroom during October. It was early in the morning, the students were just filing into the classroom, and I was speaking with the full-time classroom teacher. Suddenly, our discussion was interrupted by a wide-eyed seven year-old who exuberantly asked if they were going to the zoo that day.

The teacher appeared puzzled, and then responded that the zoo trip was scheduled for May, some seven months later. The child was crestfallen, and tearfully asked, "Then why are the busses in front of the school?"

I sized up the situation, and told the teacher that my guess was that she had informed her students at the beginning of the year that some day they would take a field trip to the zoo. She confirmed that, but stated that it would not be until near the end of the school year. We both knew that the concept of "time" to a child is not commensurate to that of an adult, and we were not surprised that the little girl would confuse the dates, but an even more important lesson ingrained itself in my mind. The child was experiencing "egocentrism." When she observed busses in front of the school, she automatically assumed that they were there for her. They were ready to take her class to the zoo. Why else would busses be in front of her school? What other possible function would they be serving? As it turns out, the busses were there to transport fifth graders to their outdoor education experience, but to one first grade child, they had no business being there unless they were available for her convenience.

In a somewhat more sophisticated manner, many adults evidence similar egocentrism. They have their agendas set, and they blithely dismiss other ideas and agendas as inferior, unreasonable, unacceptable, unthinkable, and irrational. They literally cannot grasp how someone could (intelligently) differ from them. What alien source could possibly cause someone to be so out of step?

Benign Ignorance and Offensive Arrogance

I would like to suggest two personality derivations from the question, "Why can't you be normal like me?" Let's call the first one "benign ignorance" and the second one "offensive arrogance." In other words, the former one emanates from an innocent inability to understand that normal is a relative term. What I consider normal, you may consider abnormal, odd, or weird. It is not vicious, only immature. It does not allow for different kinds of "normalcy." If I am convinced that I am normal, then any thought, idea, or suggestion which you may have which differs from my own must naturally be not normal, therefore wrong. If anything does not fit into my defined paradigms, then there is something wrong with it. Like the first grade girl mentioned above, if the bus is not there to take me to the zoo, then it has no place in the school driveway. It just doesn't make sense.

The latter expression, "offensive arrogance," is a great deal more insidious. It allows for differing thoughts and opinions, in a cognitive sense, but it dismisses them outright because if they differ from my own, they are by definition wrong. Since I cannot be wrong, conflicting ideas must be wrong. If I am the universal distributor of truth, then who can argue with me? Let's examine these two personality derivations in a bit more detail.

As stated above, benign ignorance is an innocent inability to comprehend that there may be normal behavior outside of my own tendencies. While it is not cruel, nasty, spiteful, or pejorative, it can be intolerant and bothersome in its effect. It basically says, "This issue is so cut and dried, how can anyone possibly maintain a differing viewpoint?" It is a perspective that literally cannot imagine disagreement. It is a naïve stroll through life, without any accompanying awareness of conflict or dissonance. Let me illustrate.

Take a Gander at This Goose

Recently, I was driving on a busy street in my neighborhood (three lanes eastbound, three lanes westbound, with a small divider). I was headed eastbound in the left lane, when I noticed that about 100 yards ahead of me was a goose which had successfully negotiated the westbound lanes, was crossing the divider, and was about to embark on the second half of his perilous journey across the road. As he entered my lane, I slowed down considerably, as geese are not known for their sprinting ability. This irritated the driver behind me, who could not view the goose from his perspective, so he veered around me to the right. When he spotted the goose, he too applied his brakes, as did the driver in the right lane. The ultimate sight was priceless—three lanes of traffic at a complete halt, while an unassuming goose innocently meandered across the road, completely unaware of his potential imminent death. To the goose, the road was his domain. Much larger and more powerful automobiles were non-existent in his life-space. He had nothing to fear but fear itself.

Do you know any "unconscious" geese who suffer from benign ignorance? They are not mean, just unaware. They are not haughty, just clueless. They wander through life, questioning why so many other people are out of step with them. Do you work with or socialize with or live with any of these people? In a discussion about the new ad campaign at work, they will say to you, "How can you possibly like that ad poster? It looks terrible" (Feeler) or "It just doesn't make sense" (Thinker). Because they suffer from benign ignorance, they cannot grasp the idea that someone else may see the poster from a different perspective or from another viewpoint. While they do not mean to be critical of your judgment, they really can't understand how you are able to be so out of touch in your thinking.

I'm sure you have seen pictures which reflect several different images, based on the perspective of the beholder. The one which is probably most famous is a picture which appears in most psychology textbooks. From one viewpoint, it depicts an older woman with distorted features who gives the appearance of being a witch. But from another angle, the picture is of a young and beautiful woman. The problem of benign ignorance rises when one can see only the older woman or only the younger woman. If I can see only the older woman, and you can see only the younger woman, then we have a dialogue problem. Internally, we are both saying to each other, "How can you not see what is so obvious to me?" How can you miss the blatant picture before you? I really can't understand your lack of perspective."

Have you and a friend ever looked at a cloud pattern and shared perceptions on what the cloud looks like to you? One of you thinks it looks like an elephant's trunk, while the other suggests that it looks more like a water slide or Jimmy Durante's profile. Or perhaps you see someone on television, and try to think who the person reminds you of. Both of you come up with responses which make complete sense to you, but for the life of you, you cannot vision your friend's choice. Perceptions arise not because of what things really are, but because of how we view those things.

Let me give you a more tangible example. As you turn to the next page, cover up page 55, and only look at page 54. Look at the shapes on the page. Do they make any sense to you? Do you see the word FLY within the shapes? If not, try to concentrate on the white spaces, not on the black shapes. Now do you see the word FLY? If you still cannot see it, look on page 55, where a border has been drawn around the shapes. Is it more obvious now? Can you see how benign ignorance limits our ability to understand others and the way they look at things? Can you envision how overcoming benign ignorance would improve relationships, and would assist us in eliminating the question, "Why can't you be normal like me?" Remember that we are talking about dealing with YOUs, people we relate to constantly. If our benign ignorance is a stumbling block to viewing work issues or other factors from the perspective of the YOU, then we can expect continuous frustration in the relationship, as well as ineffectiveness in solving problems and agreeing on decisions.

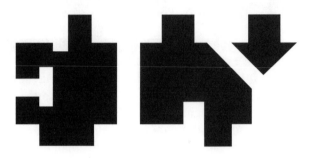

Let's talk about "offensive arrogance" for a moment. As I stated above, this one is far more insidious than benign ignorance. This one is not an innocent questioning of another's judgment, or a true inability to understand despite repeated attempts. This one represents a serious character flaw, and the possessor of offensive arrogance may well have some problems that are genuinely clinical in nature. This person has successfully convinced him or her self that he or she is head and shoulders above other people, worthy of worship, king of the hill, above the law, untouchable, and as close to perfect as one can possibly be. Some people have made an art form of arrogance, and I'm sure you know several of them. In fact, since you began reading this paragraph, I would bet you have named a couple. That is why this section is so easy to write. I just think of two or three people I know, and the words flow like Niagra Falls.

Offensive arrogance typically takes years to perfect, although some individuals tend to be quick studies. Usually, a person has risen through the ranks to attain a lofty position, and to enjoy all the amenities that go with that position, such as preferential treatment, increased income, high visibility, and occasional groveling on the part of subordinates. Eventually, the regal atmosphere gets to feeling pretty good, and the healthy self-esteem (I am as good as anyone else) is replaced by an unhealthy arrogance (I am <u>better</u> than anyone else). The next step is to emphasize the disparity in status by treating others as lesser people. This typically takes the form of condescending behavior (the "good" king) or cruel behavior (the "evil" king). In either case, and true arrogant kings use both to their advantage, the result is that they set themselves up as superior to others. Do you remember the book <u>Animal Farm</u>, by George Orwell? When the pigs took over the farm, they chortled, "All animals are equal, but some animals are more equal than others." That is the beginning of offensive arrogance.

During my college days, I worked in a men's clothing store in a rather upscale suburb of Chicago. I was young, poor, and naïve, and totally unaccustomed to the life styles of most of our customers. We had a few "favorites" who we tried to avoid like the plague because of their propensity for offensive arrogance, but on occasions we were forced to deal with them. One summer afternoon, I was the only salesman on the floor, and there were no customers at the time. One of our "favorite ladies" (in the interest of family values, I will refrain from revealing her local moniker) walked through the door, saw the almost empty store, and asked, "Isn't anyone here?" I responded, "I am," and she retorted, "I mean someone <u>important</u>!" I quickly reminded myself that both God and my mother loved me, and that I should not take offense at her comment, so I quietly informed her that all the important people were away from the store at the moment, but that I would be deliriously happy to assist her. She chose to leave and return later when someone important could provide proper assistance to someone of her status.

When it comes to, "Why can't you be normal like me," offensive arrogance is as different from benign ignorance as night and day, although it may not always be obvious, as the results can be similar or exactly the same. I choose not to dwell here on offensive arrogance for at least two reasons. First, as stated above, if you are dealing with a narcissistic personality, no amount of logic or counseling will help to solve the problem because the other person is not playing by the same rules. Actually, the other person <u>cannot</u> play by the same rules because he or she has a warped perception of relationships and is unable to view you as an equal. Most of us do whatever is in our power to avoid such individuals, and to have as few dealings with them as possible. This leads to the second reason for not dwelling on offensive arrogance, which is that, for most of us, offensive arrogance does not characterize the YOUs in our lives, as we have defined them here. The lady in the store who referred to me as unimportant was not a YOU in my life. She was a THEM in my life, and we will talk about THEMs in later chapters. Because I did not know her well (nor cared to), interacted with her on a regular basis, or shared any of my life with her, she was not a YOU to me.

My guess is that you also do not <u>knowingly</u> have YOUs in your life who are characterized by offensive arrogance. If you do, you might want to question why you feel so close to someone who regards you as a lesser person. That would probably indicate other special needs or insecurities which should be examined and treated. I use the word "knowingly" because of another possibility which I will refer to briefly, and that is our occasional inability to accurately perceive offensive arrogance. They say that love is blind, and I would broaden the definition of love to cover all types of relationships. There are times when we cannot, or choose not to, discover some serious flaws in those with whom we are extremely close. They may exhibit offensive arrogance, but because of the relationship, we do not view it as either offensive or arrogant until the situation changes, and along with it, the relationship. Let me illustrate with a true story, with the names changed to protect both the innocent and the guilty.

For a number of years, Bert worked closely with Larry, a man whose temperament and personality closely paralleled his own. As a result, they got along famously and became best of friends, or so Bert thought. They traveled a great deal in their jobs, and were together almost incessantly. Since Larry was Bert's boss, it was easy for him to make sure that Bert was well taken-care-of, which of course kept him contented, encouraged him to be more productive, and confirmed to him their sincere friendship. It was some years later that the truth hit Bert. Outwardly, they were best of friends because Bert was valuable to Larry and made him look good. Bert served a function that Larry needed in his life—someone to help make him successful, someone to have fun with, someone to confide in.

But when Larry's position changed in the organization, and he no longer needed Bert, the relationship changed dramatically. It was at that point that Bert noticed how offensively arrogant Larry had become (when in reality, he was that way all along—because of their relationship, Bert had not noticed it earlier). Bert was no longer important to Larry and, worse yet, Larry treated Bert as a non-person. Suddenly, Bert was aware that Larry had treated many others in the same way, using them until they no longer served a purpose for his ego, and then trashing them. Bert remembered comments others had made about Larry previously, which Bert had dismissed because of their friendship. He thought these other people just didn't understand Larry; actually, they understood him considerably better than Bert did. Ironically, Larry was the one who taught Bert an expression which he bought into lock, stock, and barrel: "Loyalty is number one—everything else can be bought by the yard."

Bert still believes in the truth of that expression, but over the years he came to realize that he and Larry define loyalty in drastically diverse terms. To Larry, loyalty meant blind obedience, never questioning a decision, never challenging an opinion. His concept of loyalty was vertical in nature, and one-dimensional. The "subordinate" is loyal to the "superior," but the loyalty need not be reciprocal. Loyalty is status oriented—one is obligated while the other is not. This was very difficult for Bert to accept. To him, loyalty is horizontal, and can only be truly experienced on a relational level. It means caring for the other person in all situations and at all costs. It means warning the other person if you believe that a decision will result in disaster, or challenging an opinion if you feel that it might backfire. It means, as the Bible states, "Speaking the truth in love." It transcends status or position, and it flies in the face of those who perceive themselves to be above others. Because of Larry's narcissistic personality, he would never be capable of understanding that concept of loyalty. If it did not feed into his ego needs, or provide the gratification or affirmation he desperately required, it was considered disloyal. Not surprisingly, numerous people who reported to him turned out to be "disloyal."

Having dismissed the concept of offensive arrogance in our YOUs, let's return to the more prevalent and pesky issue of benign ignorance as the cause of people not being perfect like we are. For this purpose, it might be helpful if we utilize the concept of temperament types again, as they explain tendencies and perspectives, and that is what benign ignorance is all about. Because I have a tendency to view issues, ideas, concepts, and situations from my own perspective (which I think is perfect), and because some of my YOUs (due to their tunnel vision) have a tendency to view these things from a different perspective (which I think is imperfect), we sometimes cannot understand each other, we sometimes confuse each other, we sometimes disagree with each other, and we sometimes frustrate each other. From a temperament point of view, how does this happen? Let's focus on that in the next chapter.

CHAPTER 5

◆◆◆

ARE WE SPEAKING
THE SAME LANGUAGE?

**"The more we arg'ed the question
the more we didn't agree"
– Will Carleton
Betsy and I Are Out
(quoted in *Familiar Quotations*, p. 808)**

In our quest for understanding why our YOUs suffer from benign ignorance, we look to the differences in our temperament types, trusting that it will provide insight into why these people just can't seem to get it right. They are almost there, but not quite perfect. They get it right most of the time, but not all of the time. We can agree on the majority of the issues, but every once in a while they say or do something that indicates they are not yet as perfect as we are. A deck of 51 cards will mess up the game every time, and for some reason, when the chips are down and the rubber meets the road, they cannot be counted on to see it my way. Why does the difference in temperament always seem to block our otherwise perfect communication, and prevent them from understanding why I am right? Let's begin with the extravert and the introvert.

E — I

If you recall, extraverts are people who rev up their engines by being in social situations. They tend to be energized when surrounded by other people. While they require time alone for reflection and rest, they look forward to the next gathering, and the opportunity for mingling and sharing with others. Introverts, on the other hand, are most energized by being alone, or with a select few others. Most introverts have the ability to interact with many others in a successful manner, but it is not their preferred style. They tend to become run-down by such interaction, and they long for retreat into solitude. So, which style is perfect and which one is imperfect?

Hopefully, we all agree by now that both styles are good because they are naturally ingrained in all of us. Intellectually, we can understand others who are different from the way that we are. The problems tend to arise when we encounter situations where we immediately defer to our own preferred styles, and that pull is powerful enough to cloud our sensitivities toward differing styles. To me, this is the most crucial element in this entire discussion, and I am going to say it again. The problems tend to arise when we encounter situations where we immediately defer to our own preferred styles, and that pull is powerful enough to cloud our sensitivities toward differing styles. In other words, despite all our good intentions to understand perspectives other than our own, in the heat of the moment, our inclination is to fall back on what we know and do naturally, and only later to consider the alternatives. Let me present a hypothetical scenario.

An extraverted husband decides to plan his introverted wife's 40th birthday party. His first thoughts are which restaurant to call (she would prefer home), how many people to invite (she would prefer none or a couple), what entertainment to have (she would prefer obscurity), and what surprise mini-party to follow (she would prefer going home). When they finally arrive home, he is zoomed, presents her with her birthday present (a sexy negligee which he knows she is <u>dying</u> to model), and proceeds with his elaborate love-making plans. She is exhausted, still somewhat uncomfortable with all the public attention, and desperately wants to sleep for ten hours. Draw your own conclusion as to how that evening is going to end, and who is going to be unhappy, and what the relationship will be like the following morning.

What went wrong? Which one of the two failed to understand where the other was coming from? Probably both. He is likely saying, "How can she be such an ingrate? I worked so hard to arrange all the details, to make sure it was an unforgettable time for her, to be certain she was the center of attention. I did it all for her" (and in his mind, he did). She is likely saying, "I would have much preferred a quiet dinner with just the two of us. Why does he have to make such a big deal of everything? And how can he expect me to be sexually responsive when I am drained from all the activity? He is so selfish" (and from her perspective, he is).

Think about that scenario for a few minutes. I'm sure some of you can relate to it tearfully well. While you may love that person deeply, he or she is not quite perfect because he or she just doesn't understand where you are coming from. How can that person possibly think that . . .? Why isn't he or she perfect like me?

Now let me present another example from the world of work. An introverted boss notices that Becky (an extravert) is doing an outstanding job as a staff supervisor. Becky mingles well with her people, she is a remarkable motivator, she keeps the office morale sky-high, productivity is impressive, and she is well-liked by those whom she supervises. The boss decides that Becky should be rewarded, so she promotes her to Executive Assistant, complete with a private office and her own secretary, not to mention a healthy increase in pay. She instructs Becky to eat her lunch in the executive dining room, to interact only with those on her floor, and to spend the majority of her day alone in her office, where she can be most productive in her new role. Becky, of course, detests the assignment. She envisions herself as a hermit, forced into a cloistered life against her will.

After several weeks, she tries to explain to her boss that she was much more contented when she worked with the entire steno pool staff, and that while she is grateful for the promotion, she would prefer to have her old job again. She likely says, "Why can't she understand that interaction with people means more to me than a promotion and a raise? Since I am doing a good job, why can't she allow me to continue doing well in my position? Why does she punish me like this?" Becky's boss, who also happens to be a feeler, takes the rejection personally. She likely says, "Why is Becky so naïve? Why can't she understand that I am moving her along the career path? What is wrong with her that she cannot grasp how good she has it here? And why does she try to make me look like a fool by suggesting that my decision was incorrect?" As expected, the relationship between Becky and her boss deteriorates significantly. Things go from bad to worse, and eventually Becky leaves the company.

Does that one sound familiar? Does benign ignorance have a tendency to drive a wedge between us and the YOUs in our lives? If only they would take the time to understand us better in terms of our extraverted or introverted natures. But for some reason they just don't get it. They aren't quite perfect like we are, and that is so irritating!

S — N

Can the debate end here, or do sensors and intuitors also find each other less than perfect? Remember that sensors like to name, number, and count. They are literal people, and they use their five senses to interpret information. They tend to deal with tangible things, and they usually live in the present (what is). Intuitors like to use hunches and "vibes." They are "virtual" as opposed to literal. They tend to deal with intangible things, and they visualize opportunities. They live in the future (what could be). They have a tendency toward being idealistic instead of realistic like their sensor counterparts. They are "idea" people, while sensors are "practical" people. Which of these two types is less than perfect?

A sensor and an intuitor are co-managers of a project management team at a local home improvement center, where most of the customers phone in their questions and orders. Sales have fallen off during the past six months, and customers frequently complain about the unprofessional treatment they receive by phone operators. The project management team, lead by Sandra the Sensor and Ian the Intuitor, has been commissioned to develop a "customer-friendly" training program for the phone operators, featuring elements such as etiquette, patience, helpfulness, can-do attitude, etc. Sandra and Ian agree to meet on Monday morning to initiate planning for the training program.

Ian shows up on Monday with a list of possible goals and objectives for the program, along with some ideas as to how it might be cleverly integrated into some of the training already in place at the company. He suggests that they take time to discuss their philosophy of training, in light of the particular "culture" of their organization. He wants to be sure that what they are proposing is consistent with the mission statement of the organization, and that it will be a good fit with other types of training and growth opportunities which the employees have experienced in the past.

Sandra is mildly confused, not to mention frustrated, with Ian's theoretical and philosophical approach to this assignment. She entered the meeting prepared to discuss time constraints, topics (by priority), availability of facilitators, equipment needed, scheduling, and ways to evaluate the success of the program. She expected to have all the details worked out within hours, with a final program proposal on the boss' desk by Wednesday. Ian never gave a thought as to when the proposal would be complete. He accuses Sandra of jumping the gun, putting the cart before the horse, and being more concerned with trivia (methods) than substance (concepts). Sandra accuses Ian of pie-in-the-sky nonsense, making a mountain out of a molehill, and dreaming instead of doing. It is only a project, for heaven's sake, not the development of a new society.

After much discussion, argument, hurt feelings, misunderstanding, and verbal abuse, Sandra and Ian ask for help in resolving their differences, because the other one just doesn't want to cooperate. Why do I have to put up with a person like this? Why can't he or she just get over the pig-headedness and obstinacy, and work with me to complete our assignment? Why can't he or she be perfect like me?

T — F

If you thought the extravert and introvert YOUs and the sensor and intuitor YOUs were frustrating to each other, wait until you see this pair—thinker and feeler YOUs. Call in the triage unit because blood is about to flow. The last person standing will be declared the winner, it is no place for the faint of heart, and even Elvis has left the building.

Let's refresh our memories. Thinkers are people who use logic and rationality when making decisions or forming opinions. They tend to be objective, they detach themselves personally from situations they encounter, and they try not to allow extenuating circumstances to cloud the issue. They use reason and "common sense" to guide their thought processes. Feelers are people who use emotion and subjectivity when making decisions or forming opinions. They tend to personalize situations which do not necessarily affect them. They look for extenuating circumstances to clarify issues, so that those issues do not appear sterile. They also use "common sense" to guide their thought processes, but such common sense is derived through a more emotional perspective.

The thinker often accuses feelers of being bleeding-heart liberals (if they are compassionate feelers) or vicious tyrants (if they are vindictive feelers). They wear their hearts on their sleeves, they are terribly illogical, they have no sense of standardization, they are overly sensitive, they cannot make tough decisions, and they are not fair because they swing back and forth as their moods dictate. God help us if all jurors were feelers because the most persuasive attorney would win the case, regardless of whether the accused were innocent or guilty (have we ever seen that happen in our society?).

The feeler often accuses thinkers of being cold and heartless (if they are vindictive thinkers) or boring and predictable (if they are compassionate thinkers). They are logical to a fault, they are stuck in their ways, they display no sensitivity or diversion of attitude based on the situation, they cannot "get out of the box," and they refuse to attempt to understand how other people feel about an issue. God help us if all jurors were thinkers because missionaries and terrorists would be granted the same consideration.

Very recently, I was summoned to jury duty in Chicago. I did not actually serve on a case, which was fine because of my hectic schedule, but I related to our Office Manager that I thought it would have been fascinating to sit through a trial, hear the evidence, weigh the facts, and make a decision (clearly a thinker experience). She (a feeler) responded that she would be uncomfortable making a decision that could affect another person's life in some way. After our discussion, I realized how differently we had viewed the idea of jury duty. She saw it as having the responsibility of making a decision regarding someone else's life, while I saw it as a task of sifting through evidence in order to make that decision. She thought of it as personal involvement while I thought of it as impersonal, accomplishing a task.

"I hate to do this, but I have to."
Thinker

"I hate to do this, so I won't."
Feeler

For an example of this tension, refer back to chapter 2 (page 25), where the two avid Chicago Bears fans are watching a game together. Although they are inseparable friends, they are at loggerheads on this particular Sunday afternoon. In his wildest dreams, the thinker cannot understand how his buddy could possibly root for the Lions, when a victory for Detroit would move them past the Bears into first place. Is this not a cut-and-dried issue? A good thing for the Lions is a bad thing for the Bears. Does a true Bears fan want a bad thing to happen to the Bears? Can the true Bears fan therefore root for the Lions? He is likely saying, "Hello—earth to feeler! Where is your common sense? Why are you such a moron? Why aren't you perfect like me?"

In his wildest dreams, the feeler cannot comprehend how his buddy would root for the Packers. He has <u>never</u> rooted for the Packers in his entire lifetime. How can he break the streak now? Doesn't he remember all the times the Packers beat up on his beloved Bears? Can't he visualize a muddy and bloody Dick Butkus standing firm in the trench, vowing that no lousy Packer would cross the goal line while there was breath left in the Chicago defense? He is likely saying, "What is wrong with this traitor thinker? There are still six weeks left in the season for the Bears to catch the Lions. Have faith—they will prevail. But whatever the situation, whatever the cost, you do <u>not</u> root for the Packers. How can you be so treasonous? Why aren't you perfect like me?"

If you find the above scenario to be humorous, but not terribly realistic, you are not a Chicago Bears fan. I have been a Bears fan my entire life, and I have witnessed arguments far more fierce than the one mentioned above. Come to think of it, I have been an active participant in several of them.

Let's look at another example from the world of work. Frances and Brian are co-managers of a 30 member tax division in a medium-sized company. They have been notified that they must downsize their division by 10%, which will mean a loss of three employees. They have one week to determine how to accomplish the downsizing task.

Frances (who is a feeler) and Brian (who is a thinker) approach things differently. The first thing Brian does is make a list of potential "disposable" employees, so that he can set the parameters for the task. The first thing Frances does is wonder if there might be a way around laying people off. For example, could people be shifted, or have reduced hours, or take a pay cut? She wants to explore alternative measures that would save jobs, while Brian just assumed that his task was to reduce the work force, and so he set out to do his job.

When they meet together to discuss the situation, Frances and Brian realize how their approaches have been different. Brian is frustrated that Frances wishes to explore other possibilities because it takes time away from his numerous other responsibilities. Frances is perturbed that Brian appears to be unconcerned about the "at risk" employees. He seems to be more involved with the mechanics of downsizing than he does with caring about the people whose lives are bound to be affected. Brian finally agrees to investigate alternative action plans, but only if Frances does the leg-work. She does, and after several days, comes to the disheartening conclusion that three employees must be laid off.

Frances and Brian meet again to determine who the unfortunate employees will be. Brian has a chart prepared, demonstrating which positions are most expendable, and how cross-training will help to fill in the voids. He has even completed a cost-benefit analysis for the division, which evidences the wisdom of his selections. Frances counters Brian's charts with some information of her own. She notes that one employee is only three years away from retirement (and perhaps could be offered an "early out"), that one person on Brian's "expendable" list is a single mom with four children who desperately needs her job, that another individual on the list has been with the company for 22 years (and in the past has volunteered to accept thankless jobs to keep the organization profitable), and that yet another employee on the list is extremely popular with all the other workers—keeping both production and morale at a high level.

Notice the differences in their styles. Frances becomes personally involved in the private lives and extenuating circumstances of the "at risk" employees, while Brian sticks to the facts, figures, and statistics. Brian regards the task as an impersonal part of his job which must be done like any other unpleasant duty. Frances cannot view the situation objectively because she has a relationship with the individuals involved. To her, this is far more than a business decision. Unfortunately (and here is where the blood-letting begins), Brian and Frances fail to recognize the necessity to understand each other's position, and to work cooperatively to reach a decision. Instead, they dig in their heels and mutter, "Why can't he/she be perfect like me?" Then the war begins.

Frances accuses Brian of being cold, hard, cruel, and heartless (which he probably isn't), and of not caring whether people survive or not. She refers to him as Attila the Hun and Nero wrapped up into one person. She suggests he pursue a new career in the military, where he can instigate war and indiscriminately murder without worrying about consequences. For a coup de grace, she asks how he would feel (a typical feeler question) if it were <u>his</u> mother being thrown out into the street by such an insensitive tyrant as himself.

Brian is slightly taken aback by the reference to his mother, but the rest of Frances' tirade doesn't faze him all that much. He accepts it as emotional slobbering, and attributes it to her feminine nature. He knows he should not retaliate, but the challenge is too tempting, so he sets sail on a similar attack. First, he points out (quite logically) that <u>all</u> employees are people, whether they are young, old, men, women, single parents, independent, etc. Their personal circumstances have nothing to do with their employment status. He then points out that a business decision must be made according to what is best for the division, as no individuals are more important than the unit.

Lastly, he criticizes Frances for her inability to see the big picture, and for her immature reaction to their disagreement. How can she be so unprofessional as to allow her emotions to dictate her responses to a work task? Doesn't she understand that thousands of people get laid off every day? It is a fact of life, and she needs to deal with reality. And furthermore, if she can't make a tough decision, she needs to let someone else do the job, and she can retire to the soap opera world, for which she is much better suited.

I have two questions for you. First, how do you think they finally resolved the issue as to who would be terminated? Second, what do you think their personal relationship was like from then on? Have you ever witnessed a relationship, either personal or professional, gone sour because the individuals involved just could not understand how the other one was thinking, and neither would take the time to retreat, consider another perspective, clarify values and viewpoints, or withhold judgment for the sake of honest discussion? Friends are lost and wars are started because some people just don't get it. Why can't they be perfect like me?

J — P

If all else fails, turn to the judgers and perceivers. Surely they are both perfect, aren't they? Please recall that judgers like things planned, decided, settled, completed, and closed. One of their favorite expressions is "signed, sealed, and delivered." They worship deadlines and decisiveness. Fixed routines are comfortable, while ambiguity is frightening. Plan ahead, be on time, have an agenda ready, and leave nothing to chance. Judgers may not always buy NIKE products, but they swear by the slogan, "Just do it!"

Perceivers like things flexible, tentative, open-ended, and optional. They adore continuous choices, second chances, and alternative paths. Fixed routines are stifling, while ambiguity is refreshing. Leave your options open, never burn a bridge, wait and see, and time will tell. One expression perceivers love to hear is, "If you change your mind, you can always return it for a cash refund." So who is the imperfect one, the judger or the perceiver?

For years, Jill and Len (both perceivers) have taken a week's vacation together each summer, driving to the mountains, backpacking, climbing, swimming, hiking, and generally relaxing. This year, however, they decided to vacation with their neighbors and good friends, Barb and Stuart (both judgers). The two couples met twice to "plan" the vacation, and each time Jill and Len came away a bit uneasy. It seemed as though Barb and Stuart were a little too much into the planning, and might spoil some of the spontaneity and adventure. Little did they know!

On getaway day, Barb and Stuart showed up with the camper completely stocked with supplies that would have lasted a millennium. The couples had agreed that they would spend some time at Mirror Lake, a favorite of Jill and Len's, but they failed to clarify how they would get there. Jill and Len assumed that they would meander for two days, pausing to walk and explore, visit an exotic community along the way for several hours, and picnic beside a river or in the foothills of a mountain. Barb and Stuart, however, had other ideas. They arrived at 6:00 am, with a map from AAA, explaining that it would take approximately 9 hours to get to Mirror Lake if they stopped only twice for 30 minutes each. Stuart announced that lunch was no problem, as there were a number of fast food restaurants along the way, but that they needed to make a decision regarding dinner. He asked Len if he and Jill preferred seafood or steak, as he had reservations at two different restaurants in Mirror Lake for 7:30. Either reservation could be canceled, so the decision was up to them. Len and Jill, of course, had no idea what they wanted for dinner at 6:00 am, and wondered aloud why they had to arrive at Mirror Lake that day. Stuart was clearly miffed. Naturally they had to arrive that day— why would anyone want to waste precious vacation time traveling?

As the day wore on, with Jill and Len suggesting that they stop to walk for a while and take pictures, and Barb and Stuart gazing anxiously at their watches, it became apparent to everyone that this might not be a vacation made in heaven. At one point, Stuart asked Len if he wanted to go fishing early the next morning. Len responded that he had no idea what he wanted to do the next morning, but that he would think about it. Stuart explained that the reason he had inquired was because the National Weather Service had predicted rain for later in the day, and that if they wanted to fish, it might be best to do that early. Barb added that Mirror Lake had advertised a water-skiing show on Wednesday afternoon, so they might want to arrange their agenda around that activity. She also noted that the fireworks display was scheduled for Friday night at 9:00, so she suggested an early dinner that night.

At this point in the conversation, Jill stated that she was already worn out from all the planning activity. She allowed as how a vacation to her was supposed to be relaxing, but so far she felt as if she were back at work, meeting deadlines. She suggested that they all "chill out" for a while, take each hour and day as it came, do whatever they chose to do on the spur of the moment, and truly enjoy their vacation. The final part of her comment, "and truly enjoy their vacation," hit a sore spot with Barb and Stuart. How could you truly enjoy a vacation that was not planned out? If you don't know what you want, you will miss out, and go home wishing you had seen and experienced more. If you only vacation one week each year, why wouldn't you schedule it so as to maximize your fun and pleasure?

Predictably, the remainder of the vacation became more unpleasant for everyone, further polarized the couples' definitions of fun, and drove a lasting strain in their relationship. The judgers could not comprehend how people would "waste" their vacation time in aimless activity, not enjoying every minute to the fullest. The perceivers could not comprehend how people would "stifle" themselves during vacation time, inhibiting their freedom of spirit, and turning liberating enjoyment into confining shackles.

Let me provide another example which relates to the marketplace. Dan and Robert work for Bell Graphics, and are responsible for print jobs being completed on time. They currently have a large order from their biggest client, Union Manufacturing, which is due in three days. The order is worth over $4000, which is a significant sum of money to Bell Graphics. They need to crank out the order as soon as possible. But there is a problem.

The print machine has been experiencing problems, and is in need of instant repair. As is, any print jobs will be rejected by Union Manufacturing. Dan and Robert called a repair service, which guaranteed repair of the machine within 48 hours. Today is Tuesday, the order is due on Friday, but the machine may not be attended to until Thursday. Even then, there may be an unforeseen problem preventing total repair. Maintenance will cost between $200 and $600. Dan, who is a judger, is mostly concerned that the Union Manufacturing order be completed and delivered on time regardless of cost and reduction of profit to Bell Graphics. He suggests contracting out the job to a competitor in order to guarantee completion. Robert, who is a perceiver, does not share Dan's sense of urgency. He would prefer to take a wait-and-see attitude on the repair service rather than hastily decide to contract out the order, thus reducing profit. He reasons that if the print machine is fixed by Thursday, that still leaves almost a full day to complete the job. If, for some reason, time runs out, he can explain the emergency problem to Union and request a one-day grace period.

Robert's laissez-faire attitude drives Dan crazy. He knows how crucial Union's business is to Bell, and he desperately wants to avoid angering them with a delay. He would rather forfeit some profit in order to maintain good will. He attempts to persuade Robert how important it is to have the security of a job completed. Robert isn't buying it, and he accuses Dan of being paranoid and obsessive. He assures Dan that it will all work out, and if not, they will develop a plan B that will be equally advantageous. He does not want to jeopardize the maximum profit, and he defiantly asserts that Dan's cautious attitude will cost them money.

Dan counters Robert's attack with one of his own. He accuses Robert of being short-sighted with regard to profit, and not taking the business seriously. He further states that Robert doesn't plan well or pay much attention to deadlines. In fact, if he were more conscientious, he would have insisted on regular maintenance of the print machine, and the current problem would be non-existent.

Both Dan and Robert insist that they are right, and that the other person is out of step. Their relationship is shaky because they both know for a fact that the other one just doesn't understand how to approach decision-making or problem-solving at the workplace. Why can't he be perfect like me?

Are we speaking the same language? Even though our temperaments and personalities are different, and even though we express ourselves in diverse ways, can I really appreciate the fact that we are both attempting to communicate effectively with each other? Can I somehow conquer the nagging assumption that because I don't always understand your thoughts, motivations, feelings, and statements, that does not mean that you are skill-deficient according to my perfect measuring rod? Is it possible that I am being unrealistic in terms of our relationship and communication patterns? In fact, is it possible that, due to my own mortality and potential for error, I have neglected a key element in this process? I need to step back and reassess some crucial assumptions I may have formed. It might be slightly uncomfortable, I may have to swallow some pride, and I could be subjected to some pain, but if I am committed to the YOUs in my life, it is a step that will serve me well in my quest for growth.

CHAPTER 6

Is it possible that I can guilty of being ignorance?

♦♦♦

I COULD NEVER DO SUCH
A THING AS THAT

**"Most of us don't put our best foot forward
until we get the other one in hot water"
– Arnold Glascow
(quoted in _Quote Unquote_, p. 29)**

Now I would like to make a startling and frightening leap headlong into an area where even the boldest and most intrepid of angels would fear to tread. Let me begin this perilous venture by posing the following question (with appropriate fear and trembling): Is it remotely possible, in your wildest dreams, that you and I could ever be characterized as possessing benign ignorance? So far we have concentrated on the YOUs in our lives as lacking perfection due to their inability to be on the same wavelength as we are in all situations. Now it is time to convert the microscope into a mirror, and to honestly confront the dreaded possibility that we might also occasionally demonstrate benign ignorance in our dealings with our YOUs.

After recovering from the initial shock of realizing that I might not be absolutely perfect all of the time, I should be able to re-direct my perspective in interactions with my YOUs. I can begin by eliminating the question, "Why can't you be perfect like me?" and replacing it with, "Since neither of us is perfect, how can we best attempt to understand each other, in terms of temperament, tendency, and reasoning?" This is a lot more difficult than it appears. No matter how much we desire to change, no matter how hard we try, no matter how much we practice, there will always linger the tendency to assume that our position is right, and that the person who sees things differently is imperfect.

- It is a rare driver whose first reaction is to understand that the person ahead of him or her might be lost or confused instead of being just an "idiot slow-poke."

- It is an unusually sensitive observer who gives his or her office-mate credit for handling a problem in a certain fashion which appears unorthodox rather than referring to the person as a "moron."

- It is human nature to assume that I am always right, and to judge others on the basis of my own logic or feelings. It takes continuous and concentrated effort to remove myself from the throne of perfection, and to desire to truly understand and appreciate the differences in others.

I guess I'm not perfect after all. Once I thought I made a mistake, but I was wrong.

A couple of years after I graduated from college, I learned that someone who had been a friend when we were in school had held a protest at the institution, and had publicly burned his diploma. I was not aware of what his protest was all about, nor why he chose to take the actions he did. In fact, I had not spoken with him since graduation. Someone questioned me about the incident, hoping that I would condemn the action. I responded something like this: "I don't know what the protest was about, but I know the person involved, and I trust him and his motives. Until I am proven wrong, I will support him in whatever action he takes." He heard about my comments, and called to thank me for my statement and my support. He said it was gratifying to have my trust and my backing. I am glad I took the stance I did, and it makes me ask myself, "Why can't I <u>always</u> be that way?" Why can't I naturally assume goodness and appropriate behavior for the YOUs in my life? If I am going to make a mistake, I would rather make it by overly-trusting than by overly-judging. The throne of perfection does not wear my nameplate.

Let's assume that we recognize our imperfections, that we understand and respect the temperament differences in the YOUs in our lives, and that we wish to avoid holding their actions and beliefs to our own implied standards. Now what? How can we reflect our philosophy in behavior? When the chips are down, decisions need to be made, and in the heat of the moment, how can we act in such ways so as to demonstrate our understanding and acceptance of the differences between ourselves and our YOUs? Allow me to suggest eight points on the sign that will help to **STOP** the urge to assume benign ignorance on the part of others, and instead to consider situations from their perspective, as well as from my own.

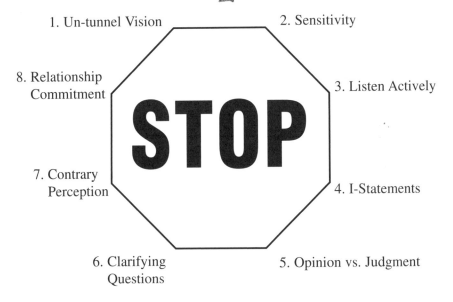

1. Un-tunnel Vision
2. Sensitivity
8. Relationship Commitment
3. Listen Actively
7. Contrary Perception
4. I-Statements
6. Clarifying Questions
5. Opinion vs. Judgment

As the old song goes, "It takes two to tango." Well, it also takes two to tangle, and if I make a conscious effort to stop the urge to assume benign ignorance on the part of others, then I might successfully eliminate my contributions to the tangling which so often characterizes our relationships. I'm sure these are not the only eight ways to combat the problem, but I've seen them work in numerous situations, and I offer them as options for consideration.

1. Un-Tunnel the Vision

In previous chapters, we talked about tunnel vision, the inability to see things from the perspective of another. What makes tunnel vision so difficult to recognize and correct is that it is almost imperceptibly subtle, and inherent in all of us. If I experience physical blurred vision or have a problem with depth perception, it causes me a certain amount of dysfunction, and therefore it is screamingly obvious to me that I need help from a trained professional. Only by correcting the problem can I regain the vision necessary to be functional in my day-to-day activities. But this is not typically the case with psychological tunnel vision. Because it is inherent in me, and because it is so subtle, it causes me no pain or discomfort, and therefore, I don't realize that anything is wrong. When was the last time, in the middle of a good day when you were feeling great, that you suddenly said to yourself, "I really should see a doctor?" Probably not recently. We don't think about physical examinations when we are feeling wonderful. And we don't usually question whether or not we have tunnel vision because it is the way we <u>always</u> look at things, and it feels so right.

Therein lies the problem! It is a life-long habit, and it feels right. Contrary to physical eyesight, which self-corrects when we suddenly switch from looking at a close object to looking at a far away object, changing tunnel vision requires a conscious decision, one which most of us never even think about making. Because we are locked into our own unique way of viewing life and its circumstances, we tend to interpret all events and activities from that perspective only. It is an unconscious act, as are most habits, and we typically do not question whether our interpretations are good or bad, or right or wrong. They are inherently good and right because they are ours. Can you see how tunnel vision is so difficult to recognize? It is as natural as breathing, walking, or eating chocolate cake. It just feels so good.

In chapter four, I mentioned how the subway system in Chicago illustrates the limitations of tunnel vision. Let me expand on that for a moment because the rapid transit metaphor is a beautiful example of the liberating power of "un-tunneling." When I was a kid, I used to regularly ride the subway to Wrigley Field to watch the Cubs lose to whomever they were playing that day. As the train sped through the "Loop," there wasn't a whole lot to look at, but about halfway between downtown and Wrigley Field, the train began to incline, and faint sunshine appeared ahead. Soon we were at ground level, and I could see out the window. But the best part came next. We didn't stay at ground level—we kept rising until we were at second-story level. The train had been transformed from a subway to an elevated ("L") train. The scenery changed dramatically. All of a sudden, I could see three or four blocks away. In fact, I could see Wrigley Field in the distance, and my excitement built as I anticipated the ball game.

What had happened to my tunnel vision that was so dark and boring? It gave way to a panoramic view of people and buildings and cars, and it allowed me the opportunity to view dozens of scenes which I had not been able to see only a few minutes earlier.

The same is true for our psychological tunnel vision, but with one exception. The train doesn't take us there automatically. We have to make a conscious decision to ascend from the tunnel to the elevated, and most people don't do that. And the reason they don't do that is because it never occurs to them to challenge their preconceptions, or to imagine that their opinion or answer might not be the only correct or valid one. Because of a lack of effort or awareness, they remain in the tunnel, where the view is always the same.

Think about this scenario for a minute. On the evening news, you see the face of a 23-year-old man who has been arrested for a serious crime, such as rape or homicide. He looks rough and mean. What is your initial reaction to the story? Is he already guilty? Have you already condemned him? Or think about this one. Some people you know have a teen-aged daughter who has become pregnant. The parents have stated that they will support the daughter (both emotionally and financially) in any decision she makes regarding keeping the baby or not, getting married or not, etc. Have you already formed an opinion about the parents (either good or bad) without knowing anything about their values or struggles? Are people benignly ignorant because they do not conform to your vision of the ways things are, or ought to be? Un-tunneling is a difficult, yet crucial, step toward eliminating the assumption of benign ignorance in others.

2. Be Sensitive

While un-tunneling is a formidable task, let's assume that we have discovered the skill of accomplishing it, and are able to practice it in our daily dealings with others. The next step is to become sensitive toward the ways in which others perceive events and situations. Remember that the YOUs in our lives are not strangers or casual acquaintances; rather, they are people who are near and dear to us in any number of ways, and therefore, the desire to be sensitive to them should be present. This, of course, is easier said than done. We can state that we are aware and sensitive to how others view issues and circumstances, and we can try admirably hard to do so, but until we master the art, there will always be a tendency to resort to our tunnel vision in the heat of the moment. How we interact with our YOUs when the chips are down and our pride is on the line demonstrates how high we have scaled the sensitivity ladder.

Simon says, "Be sensitive."

Do you remember when you were a kid, and you played a game called, "Simon Says?" For those of you who find it difficult to recall youth, here is a brief synopsis. The leader would instruct you to perform certain physical acts (touch your right knee, turn to the left, take one step backward, etc). You were only allowed to follow the instruction if the leader prefaced the command with, "Simon says. . ." If you inadvertently followed the instruction without being told to do so by "Simon," then you had to drop out, and the last kid remaining was declared the winner. The game became really fun and challenging when the leader barked out the instructions in rapid succession. He or she would give seven or eight "Simon says" instructions, and then throw in one without "Simon's" permission. I don't remember any more about the game because I was usually gone by then. But I do remember that it was fun, although my supervisors have always been bothered by the fact that I cannot follow instructions without being told to by "Simon." Simon says turn in your report next week. Oh well, some habits die hard.

To me, becoming truly sensitive to the YOUs in my life is a lot like playing "Simon Says." I may know <u>how</u> to do it, and I may really <u>want</u> to do it. But actually performing the way I want to on a consistent basis when I am emotionally invested in the issue at hand—that is another story. My tendency is to lapse back into my traditionally preferred mode, which is to understand only how I approach issues, how I think about them, how I cannot possibly be wrong or off base, and to wonder why this YOU in my life can't be perfect like I am.

Being sensitive means <u>really</u> trying to understand where the other person is coming from, rather than <u>saying</u> I am trying to understand, and then evaluating and judging the other person according to my own preconceived ideas, values, and perceptions. It means literally putting myself into the other person's skin, to actually "become" that person in order to understand how I can best relate.

Recently, I watched a made-for-TV movie about a six year old black girl (true story) who was chosen to integrate an all-white elementary school in the 60s. The behavior of the dissident white parents in the community was incredibly deplorable, and one could not help feeling intense sympathy for this innocent child who was subjected to taunts and threats which most of us have never faced in adult life, let alone childhood. I found myself asking, "How can I, a 52 year old white male, identify with what this child endured?" I can try to be sensitive, but I cannot really identify with the fear and rejection because I have never experienced the intensity of being hated because of my physical appearance. At one point in the movie, the girl refused to eat her lunch or dinner. Her parents and others who loved her cajoled her and pointed out the necessity of eating to uphold her strength. What they did not realize until later was that one of the threats she heard every day walking up the stairway to school was, "I will poison you!" If you heard that from someone who you felt was serious, how would it affect your appetite? Being sensitive means "understanding" the other person, even when you cannot really "understand" the other person.

> *Knowing where you were yesterday helps me*
> *to understand where you are today*
> *and to picture where you will be tomorrow.*

The more experienced I get at life (which is a euphemism for getting older), the more I value life experience as a legitimate reason for being sensitive to others who may be different from me. One evening, I was conducting an exercise with my adult students regarding a value judgment they had to make. I gave them a list of 21 well-known people, and their task was to choose which 6 of them would receive life-saving transplants (the others would die). The list included political, religious, and national leaders, as well as entertainers and sports figures.

One of my students, a 26 year old man (youngest in the class) tenaciously insisted on saving the life of one of the lesser-known entertainers, even at the expense of some individuals who had dedicated their lives to bettering humankind, from a social, political, or spiritual perspective. When I questioned his decision later, he explained that he had spent months in a hospital as a youth, and his only contact with the outside world was TV, and that the comedians and entertainers on TV had provided him with the impetus and stamina needed to survive his medical ordeal. From his experience, they were the heroes whose lives should be preserved. Personally, I don't watch those shows, and most TV entertainment to me is a colossal waste of time (not to mention a conflict with my values), but how do I argue with this man? I have never lived the experiences he has lived.

Being sensitive to the YOUs in our lives is a great deal more complicated and involved than the space I have afforded it here, but this is a start to get our minds and attitudes focused on stopping the tendency to assume benign ignorance on the part of others.

3. Listen Actively

This is undoubtedly the most critical and difficult step on the STOP sign (why are the most important things always the hardest to achieve?), but if one learns to successfully un-tunnel and be truly sensitive, and if one perfects the ability to actively listen, then the rest of the steps are merely procedures to getting it right. Please concentrate on this one. It will make all the difference in the world as you relate to the significant YOUs in your life.

> *Listening would be a lot easier if we could talk while we were doing it.*

What is active listening, and is the opposite of active listening "passive" listening? Well, actually, yes, although I would contend that it is not really listening at all, but rather hearing in a vague sort of way. Those of us who are parents can identify with this in a most impressive way. If you tell your child to: a) clean up his room and; b) get ready for his birthday party, can you guess which command he will hear in a vague sort of way, and which command he will actively listen to? Kids have absolutely perfected the art of selective listening. Through experience, they intuitively know which parental messages should go in one ear and out the other and which ones should be retained somewhere between the ears. I was visiting with a good friend one day, and the two of us were sitting and talking with each other and his 18 year-old son. At one point, the boy's mother began instructing him about something which has totally escaped me. She was in another room, and therefore, was speaking rather loudly. After a few minutes, she appeared in the doorway and, with a great deal of frustration in her voice, declared, "You haven't listened to <u>one</u> word I've said." He calmly responded, "Not since I was 15."

The word "listen" is derived from two ancient words which mean to hear and to wait in suspense. In other words, listening is an active experience. It is the act of tuning in to what the speaker is saying, both verbally and non-verbally. It is the eager and suspenseful awaiting to receive what the speaker has to impart. With that in mind, how often do you "listen" to your spouse, children, friends, associates, boss, coach, minister (or priest or rabbi), teacher, mentor, neighbor, news commentator, client, or anyone in general? I am not going to dwell on this at length because it has been a topic for entire books, and we could not possibly do it justice here within the limits of our scope. But let me emphasize that active listening is one of the most crucial points on the stop sign of assuming benign ignorance. If I vaguely "hear" what the other person is saying, I will miss the point and contaminate the dialogue because I will be too busy judging, rehearsing my response, and entrenching myself in my position and opinion. If I truly "listen" to what is being said, I will notice not just the words, but also the intensity of the message, and the spirit of the person who is speaking.

4. Use I-Statements

A woman turns in a report at work, and her boss responds, "You make me so mad because you never listen to me. I said I needed the report <u>last</u> week."

A wife berates her husband by exclaiming, "You never affirm me in my life goals. You only want to keep me down so you can feel better about yourself."

A father demonstrates his exasperation with his son or daughter by shouting, "You are incredibly ungrateful. Mom and I provide everything for you, but you never volunteer to help out around the house. All you do is take, take, take."

A secretary confronts her co-worker by stating, "Mary says you were ridiculing me because of my out-of-style clothes. Well, I am a single mom. I don't have a double income like you do. So quit being so snobbish!"

Do any of those tirades sound familiar? Can you identify with any of them, or even add some of your own? Such explosions assume benign ignorance (or worse) on the part of others, even though the anger involved may be completely justified. The choice of words, the tone of voice, and the accusatory implication will go a long way toward inviting a defensive reaction from the other person. This, in turn, will elicit an angry response, and some sort of a shouting match will ensue. Both parties will be angry and hurt, and the relationship will be damaged to some degree. The approaches taken above are perfect for venting frustration, but if the goal is to actually communicate and resolve an issue, they are guaranteed to fail. They will only exacerbate the problem (short-term) and widen the communication gap (long-term). There must be a better way.

I become offended when you don't use I-Statements.

Before we talk about what I-Statements are, let's take a moment to be certain we know what they aren't. I-Statements are not merely a re-wording of the accusation so as to include the word "I." For example, consider the expression, "You are stupid!" You would not convert this into an I-Statement by asserting, "I say you are stupid!" That does little to disguise the intent of the statement, and unless the person is really stupid beyond repair, he or she will mentally receive the message in the same vein as if you had left it as a You-Statement: "You are stupid!"

The purpose of making an I-Statement is to defray a defensive reaction by not attacking or accusing another person, and to make sure that the other person hears how you feel about the issue at hand. This is why it works better with the YOUs in your life. Presumably they care about how you feel, and if you are effective at communicating the feelings to them, they should be more receptive than others will be who you really do not know. The other purpose of an I-Statement is to generate a discussion about a particular issue, and to keep the focus of the dialogue on the issue itself, not on how best to "zap" the other person, and make him or her feel worthless and guilty.

I-Statements assume a level of trust between individuals, and they also assume that there is a relationship between those individuals which is worthy of preserving and enhancing. Therefore, the statements are made in order to make the other person aware that there may be a problem, that you have some rather strong feelings about the problem, and that you would like to achieve resolution to the problem in such a way so as to not inflict any violence on the relationship, but rather to respect and reinforce it.

Let's take a look back at the four scenarios we read at the beginning of this section to provide some counsel for the frustrated individuals who chose to use You-Statements to get their points across. In the first example, the boss made several mistakes:

1. "You make me so mad." No one can make us mad. We choose to be mad.
2. "You never listen to me." Highly unlikely.
3. "You." A You-Statement.

For the time being, let's just deal with the You-Statement. In order to deal with the issue and preserve the relationship, the boss could have said, "I become frustrated when you do not meet deadlines, and I perceive it as a listening problem. We need to talk about. . ."
Do you see how the attack dog is not unleashed, but the message is still clear? Obviously, if the problem is a continuing one, some other corrective action may be necessary.

In the second example, an effective I-Statement might be, "My self-esteem suffers terribly when you belittle my goals and aspirations, and I feel like I don't have your support in my efforts to grow and blossom. Why do you think you react the way you do?" Notice how she did not accuse him of an inferiority complex ("You only want to keep me down so you can feel better about yourself"), and at the same time informed him as to how he was contributing to her own inferiority complex.

The father in the third scenario might have approached his son or daughter by saying, "I feel used and taken advantage of when you assume that all the work to be done around the house falls to your mom and me. Since we all benefit from what we have, how do you suppose that we as a family might distribute the house tasks equitably? Let's talk about that." Kids are used to being "yelled at" by parents, or at least ordered around and told what to do all the time. Notice how the father shared his own frustration in an honest manner, and included the son or daughter in the decision-making process in terms of how to resolve the issue.

In the fourth example, the secretary might confront her co-worker (in private, not in public) by stating, "I feel put-down when you remark about the fact that my clothes are not the latest style. It is very difficult to make ends meet when you are a single mom like I am. Please try to be understanding about my situation. I want to know that I am judged on my character, not my wardrobe." Do you see how she avoided the accusation ("you were ridiculing me"), the comparison ("I don't have a double income like you do"), and the attack ("so quit being so snobbish")? She remained professional, dignified, and classy. She also, in a subtle way, made the other secretary realize that she was being a petty heel. I love it!

Will I-Statement approaches solve all the problems and assure that the communication remains at a high level in every scenario? Of course not, for any number of reasons, one of which is that people will always hear what they want to hear. And if they want to hear "attack" even from an I-Statement, they will respond defensively, protect their egos, and miss the opportunity to problem-solve in a mature way. But which kind of statement (I or You) do you think has a greater chance of increasing the communication and preserving the relationship?

5. Use Opinions Instead of Judgments

This one follows closely on the heels of "Use I-Statements," in that it attempts to diffuse defensive or angry responses by wording comments so as to not attack the other person or make him or her feel picked on. There are very few people in this world who enjoy having other people make them feel like dirt, and most of us tend to retaliate, either verbally or physically or both, when we are cornered or when our self-images are threatened. So if we wish to take one more step to STOP assumptions of benign ignorance, we should consider framing our thoughts as opinions or questions rather than judgments.

What do I mean by this? I mean that we should step out of the role of authority, and into the role of equal. With the YOUs in our lives, we improve and extend our relationships by sharing our opinions and feelings rather than our pronouncements and judgments. Let me give you an example. Think of a YOU in your life. What if that person said to you, "That was a mistake. You shouldn't have done that"—what would your reaction be? If you had weighed your decision carefully, and believed that you had done the best you could have done, how would you feel about the comment? Would it have made you feel less defensive or angry if the person would have said, "I don't think I agree with what you did, but maybe I don't understand why you did it; tell me what went into your thinking?"

Do you see how the first response was a judgment, while the second response was an opinion? Judgments are final, they assume authority, and they do not expect or desire feedback. Opinions, on the other hand, are meant to give input or feedback. They do not assume authority or absolute infallibility, and they leave the door open for further discussion. That is why, in the above example, a natural follow-up to "I don't think I agree with what you did, but maybe I don't understand why you did it" would be the expression "Tell me what went into your thinking." The one offering the opinion is suggesting that a dialogue may be in order, whereas the one issuing the judgment is announcing that the issue is settled, and he or she is right!

---

*"Express an opinion, but send
advice by freight."*
– Charles Clark Munn
(quoted in Quotable Quotes, p. 129)

If you look back to the beginning of this chapter, I shared a story about a friend from college who had burned his diploma in protest. I refused to criticize or judge him because he was a YOU in my life, and I trusted him. I certainly did not understand why he chose the action he did, nor did I condone it. But I did not feel as though I were in a position to judge him. That would be an authoritarian act, and that was not my place or privilege. As an equal, all I could do was offer an opinion, and hope for an explanation.

A friend wearing a new dress approaches you and asks, "How do you like my new outfit?" You believe it is unbecoming and not very flattering. You want to speak the truth. How will you state your reaction? You could say, "It does not look good on you. Those colors do not match well." Or you could say, "I personally do not like the way you look in that because. . ." In the first response, you are setting yourself up as the national design evaluator, while in the second response, you are offering a solicited opinion to a friend. Maybe the dress combined red and green, and you personally have never liked that combination (you must be a real joy at Christmas time). Obviously, that would affect your reaction to the dress. But that does not mean that red and green are a <u>bad</u> combination. Other people may absolutely adore red and green dresses. If beauty is in the eye of the beholder, then the beholder must understand that he or she does not possess a monopoly on truth or beauty.

Gentlemen, have you ever looked at the wife of a friend and wondered what he ever saw in her? One day, he shows you a recent family picture, points to his wife, and asks, "Isn't she totally gorgeous?" I would suggest you be real careful here, in terms of both judgment <u>and</u> opinion (particularly if he outweighs you by a considerable amount, or if he has just read his mail and is holding a letter opener). In this case, diplomacy and creativity are required, but be aware that judgment is definitely the wrong way to go. If you were to say the words, "Frankly, she reminds me of Miss Piggy having a bad hair day," those might be the last words you ever utter.

Let me take this one step further, and while this would not bother everyone, it can come across negatively to those who are quite sensitive regarding judgments and opinions. What I am talking about is affirming or positive judgments. While these sound good, they still imply authority, and they leave the door open for later criticism or judgment. For example, you read an article written by a friend or colleague, and you enthusiastically praise the person by stating, "This is very good! You have done an outstanding job here." Most people would bask in the adulation, while some may think, "I'm thrilled with the positive reaction, but if he or she had not approved of the article, would he or she have told me that it was terrible, hollow, and totally devoid of merit?"

By stating an opinion rather than a judgment, you remove yourself from the position of authority, and you share with your YOU what he or she asked for in the first place—what do you think? Would it not be better to respond, "I think you have done a fine job with this article, and I think you should submit it for publication. Even though I am not an expert in the area, I especially like how you explained. . ." The response is so much more personal, meaningful, and "peer" like. Incidentally, what would it do to your credibility if you told your friend that the article was outstanding, and the editors wrote back, stating that it was "terrible, hollow, and totally devoid of merit?"

Opinions help to STOP the tendency to assume benign ignorance because they recognize that I am not the appointed authority in life as to what is good or bad, beautiful or ugly, right or wrong, appropriate or inappropriate. I do not have the right to place judgment on your ideas or decisions. I only have the right to express my opinions, and then to solicit feedback so we truly understand each other.

6. Ask Clarifying Questions

Kathy and Bob are speaking about some friends of theirs, Emily and Eric, who are married, but experiencing some difficulty in their relationship. Kathy states, "Emily is about ready to walk out. She told Eric that if he doesn't start treating her with more respect, and paying more attention to her, she's gone." Bob responds, "Well, Eric has certainly heard <u>that</u> enough times." How does Kathy interpret that comment? She could have blown up and shouted, "Are you calling my friend a nag? Do you think she enjoys harping on him about his constant insensitivity? You men are all alike. Listen Buster, if you think. . ." Take a wild guess as to how Kathy and Bob will be relating to each other in about 15 minutes.

But that is not how Kathy responded to Bob's comment that, "Well, Eric has certainly heard <u>that</u> enough times." What she actually said was, "I'm not sure what you're saying. What do you mean?" Bob explained, "Emily has told Eric repeatedly that he tends to ignore her and treat her as less than an equal. If the message does not sink in to Eric pretty soon, he will have some heavy-duty problems on his hands." At that point, Kathy and Bob had a stimulating and productive conversation about their friends, and relationships in general.

What was the deciding factor between the explosion that could have been, and the dialogue that actually occurred? Kathy, instead of assuming that Bob was saying what she thought she heard, asked a clarifying question. She resisted the urge to "know" what he was thinking, preferring to allow him to explain what he was "really" thinking. In so doing, Kathy maintained the healthy relationship between Bob and herself, and she paved the way for them to converse in a meaningful and productive way.

> ### *"Exactly what part of 'NO' don't you understand?"*
> *– Anonymous*

To ask a clarifying question is to recognize that I might not be quite as clairvoyant as I wish I were, to understand that I am occasionally in error with regard to my intuitive powers. To ask a clarifying question is to admit that I possess tunnel vision, and that somewhere outside of my own experience and focus, someone might be thinking along a different track. In other words, clarifying questions reflect that I am only human—hardly a humbling admission. But how often do we automatically and immediately react and retort because we unconsciously assume benign ignorance on the part of the YOU with whom we are interacting at the time? If he said this, he must mean that!

Think of all the times recently when you were in a conversation with another person where one of you made a statement that could have been taken several ways. How did the "hearer" react? Did the person expound or lash out because of the assumption of what was meant by the statement, or did he or she ask a clarifying question in order to truly understand what was meant?

There is a priceless story I remember from many years ago which may help to illustrate how we might ask clarifying questions to assist us in understanding how to respond to the YOUs in our lives when they speak with us in terms that are not clearly understood. A seven-year-old boy asked his mother, "Where did I come from?" She sat him down, opened up a manual on sexual reproduction, explained in the most gentle way she could about intercourse, gestation, umbilical cords, and breast-feeding. When she had concluded with her quasi-medical lecture, she asked, "Does that help to answer your question about where you came from?" He responded, "Not really. My friend Dennis said he came from Boston. I just wondered where **I** came from." Asking clarifying questions can sometimes conserve a lot of energy, as well as saving us from embarrassing situations.

In this regard, I need to share one more story, a true one which happened to me. When my twin boys were in fifth grade, they made a two-day trip to the state capital with their class. They were accompanied by their school principal, who I will call Mrs. Blake. Several days after their return, I asked the boys to tell me about their trip. One of the things they related was that when they went to breakfast at the hotel, Mrs. Blake joined them, and she looked like a whore. I immediately thought about what my own parents would have done to me had I ever used a word like that (hanging by the fingernails, being grounded for decades), and I determined that I would not over-react. In fact, I decided to make this a learning experience. So I asked a question (unfortunately, not a clarifying question). I queried, "Do you know what a whore is?" I then proceeded to explain the derivation of the term, the kinds of things that whores do, the motivation (money), and the moral implications. At one point my one son interjected (no kidding), "I thought that was a hooker." So I explained that "hooker" was a slang term for whore, harlot, prostitute, etc.

I then decided to go one step further in the lesson for the day, so I asked them if they knew how to spell whore (figuring that they would not know about the "w" at the beginning of the word). At that point, Michael spelled out "h-o-r-r-o-r." I still didn't catch on and responded, "No, that word is horror." He said, "That's what I said, Dad. Mrs. Blake's hair was all messed up, and she looked like a horror." Oops! I may have had more humiliating moments in my life, but I don't remember any of them. I did learn a lesson, however. I was extremely proud of the fact that I did not react with anger or self-righteousness, but not so terribly proud of the fact that I did not ask a clarifying question.

7. Look for Contrary Perceptions

I emerge from a meeting extremely frustrated and irritated because of what transpired at the conclusion of the session. I suggested a solution to a problem which has surfaced repeatedly, and I urged immediate acceptance of my solution, as time is of the essence. It was a well-thought-out idea, and I have every confidence that it would eliminate the problem once and for all. My co-worker "stonewalled" my solution, stating that she could not approve any proposal without taking time to think over the ramifications, and the long-term effect. Then she turned to me and declared, "This is so typical of you. It seems like you are constantly coming up with ideas and proposals which you expect everyone else to rubber stamp, without giving them a chance to reflect, ask questions, and explore alternatives. It is a presumptuous and unprofessional habit."

Because my co-worker is a YOU in my life, and because I have tunnel vision and I am right all the time, she is guilty of benign ignorance. She does not understand how hard I work. She is unappreciative of the fact that I am constantly thinking about my job, and how to do it better. She is probably a little bit envious about my creative approach to problem solving, and she is bound and determined not to give me the satisfaction of her approval until she has "punished" me by making me wait for her assent. I am not really angry with her, but I am frustrated by her lack of teamwork, and the fact that she has to play these silly games of one-upsmanship. She is benignly ignorant because she is not perfect like me.

Because I am making a valiant attempt in my life to truly understand my YOUs, I determine to un-tunnel my vision, be sensitive to my co-worker, and listen actively. I know that the chances are slim and none that it is _me_ who is benignly ignorant, but in the interest of self-growth, I am willing to consider the possibility. So I make some I-Statements (at least to myself). I state, "I am frustrated when I am criticized for planning ahead and creating solutions to problems. I become upset when my co-worker impedes progress at work in order to protect her fragile ego."

You will notice here that my statements, while they appear as authentic I-Statements, still contain judgment and innuendo. I am still assuming that with regard to the issue at hand, I am definitely right and she is _most_ definitely wrong. So my next step is to clearly differentiate between my opinions and my judgments. Instead of asserting that she has a fragile ego, is unappreciative and envious, and impedes progress, I step back to analyze the situation from my own opinionated perspective. I _think_ her ego comes into play, but that is my opinion, and not an objective fact. I _think_ she is unappreciative and envious, but I cannot know how she really feels inside. I _think_ she impedes progress, but that is only how I view it. Perhaps she and others define progress as moving methodically so as to avoid rushing to judgment or implementing a decision which could be a disastrous one.

My next step is to ask clarifying questions. Since I am not with my co-worker at the moment, I will ask them hypothetically of myself. What does she mean when she states that my behavior is typical of the way I approach decision making? Does she mean I am isolated in my thinking patterns? Does she mean I don't trust the opinions of others? Does she mean I think I am the only qualified person to reach an intelligent conclusion? When she states that I don't give people a chance to reflect and consider alternatives, does she think I am seeking all the glory for good decisions? Does she think I push for immediate approval because I am trying to cover something up? When she accuses me of being unprofessional, does that mean she thinks I am not a team player? These are all questions which I need to honestly address, instead of continuing to assume that she is just benignly ignorant, and therefore I should just ignore her, or do an end-run around her whenever a decision needs to be made. This leads me to the current focus.

Do I look like the kind of person who would do that?

After I have asked my clarifying questions, I want to actually put myself in her shoes, and look for contrary evidence. In other words, I want to seek for incidences in my past behavior which might validate her comments, concerns, and accusations. As best as I can, I want to objectively exit my body and psyche, to look at myself from the outside, in order to determine whether or not I might be the one who is benignly ignorant in this situation. This is terribly difficult to do, both procedurally and psychologically (especially psychologically, as it leaves me quite vulnerable). But I am committed to the concept, so here I go. As I reflect on past meetings, do I recall pushing for immediate acceptance of my ideas, without consideration for others in the room who may have different learning and thinking styles? Do I tend to dominate brainstorm sessions, giving others the impression that I think my ideas are the only valuable ones? Do I reflect poor listening skills? Do I inadvertently emit a spirit of superiority among my co-workers? These are not easy questions to ask because they involve my ego and my self-esteem. They cut to the heart of who I am, and it is possible I don't really want to know the answers to those questions.

Let me bring this a little closer to home. Forget the workplace for a moment, and let's concentrate on our inner lives. A trusted YOU in my life has confronted me about my tendency toward holding grudges and being unforgiving. I have covered the entire gamut, from tunnel vision (he or she has no idea how badly I was hurt), to actively listening (this YOU really cares about me, and is trying to help me become a better and happier person), to making I-Statements (I resent my YOU not understanding that I lost my self-esteem and my nerve because of what happened to me, and I find it almost impossible to even think about forgiveness), to expressing an opinion instead of a judgment (I do not like my YOU insisting that I confront this issue, but that does not mean that he or she is insensitive or critical or obnoxious), to asking clarifying questions ("Why is this an issue for you? Do you believe I have been unforgiving toward you, or someone else who is close to both of us?"), to looking for contrary perceptions (do I really demonstrate this behavior on a regular basis? Can I make a list of people against whom I hold grudges, and toward whom I am unforgiving? Is it possible that my YOU is correct in his or her perception? Is there evidence to support my benign ignorance?)

As I stated in the above paragraph, the contrary evidence questions are ones I might not want to ask because of what the answers might indicate. But here is where I must make a monumental decision. If I choose to discard the mirror for fear of what I might see in it, that is okay, but I must simultaneously admit that all the rest of my efforts in this regard are a total charade. If this is where I want to exit the highway, then I need to realize that my song has been tuneless all along, and it is time to quit singing. It might be easier, and a whole lot less painful, to revert to the position of assuming benign ignorance on the part of all the YOUs in my life who disagree with me. But if true growth is my goal, then I need to include this point on the STOP sign.

8. Commit to the Relationship

The final point on the dot-to-dot octagon is a commitment (or possibly a re-commitment) to the relationship with my YOU, regardless of what that relationship might be. It is the conscious declaration that this YOU is important to me in some way. It is the confirmation that I wish to retain and strengthen the relationship, even if there is a cost to do so. If I do not feel that way, then I need to reconsider whether or not the person is really a YOU in my life. Perhaps I have always thought the person to be a YOU to me because of the frequency of our interaction, or because I was expected to think that way, but upon reflection, I actually think the individual is more of a THEM than a YOU. At that point, I will probably take a detour, but for now, let us concentrate on those relationships which are truly YOUs in our lives.

After I have cycled through the first seven points of the STOP sign, I confirm my relationship to the YOU. Hopefully by now, I have unmistakably understood that he or she does not suffer from benign ignorance. I trust that my travel experience around the STOP sign has caused me to view the situation from various perspectives, and to recognize the possibility that it is I who may be benignly ignorant. Perhaps I realize that by asking clarifying questions, or by seeking contrary evidence, I recognize that my YOU has valid perceptions, and I welcome them because my own views are broadened, and I see where I have been at least partially blind, due to my tunnel vision. Or perhaps I maintain that my YOU, despite his or her strong relationship with me, is still lacking in understanding of my feelings, experiences, and views. As I focus on the possibilities, it may dawn on me that in reality, neither of us is benignly ignorant—we just have different lenses in our glasses, due to our temperaments, values, experiences, ambitions, and inner selves. This is the point where I commit to the relationship.

> ## *"My best friend is the one who brings out the best in me."*
> ## *– Henry Ford*
> ### *(quoted in <u>Quote Unquote</u>, p. 125)*

If the issue at hand is trivial or inconsequential, I might be well-advised to ignore or forget it, as it is not worth jeopardizing the relationship, even for a short time. If the issue is meaningful or critical, or if I believe that the dialogue between my YOU and me is important for assisting us in understanding each other better, then I will want to pursue the issue. But here is where I will proceed with great caution, loving care, and a more mature and enlightened attitude than I did at the beginning of this chapter. Here is where I choose to "lose" the dreaded assumption of benign ignorance. Here is where I bury my tunnel vision ("You don't understand. I know! Why can't you get it right?") Here is where I affirm the person and the relationship, and engage in honest and equal discussion, without either of us assuming a higher position.

How does this work? How does this flesh out in daily interactions? Let's return to the scene of the crime (why can't you be perfect like me?). We stated that YOUs are pretty good people with whom we get along, but they make the fatal mistake of not sharing all of our tendencies and perspectives, and therefore, they still drive us crazy on occasions. After I have toured the STOP sign, I commit myself to the relationship I have established with my YOU, and I determine that any interchange between us will be healthy, honest, and will do no violence to our treasured "connectedness." Let me suggest an example of how I might commit to a relationship with my spouse or significant partner or friend.

As a situation arises which prompts me to have benign ignorance thoughts, and why can't you be perfect like me perceptions, I say to myself, "I respect this person, not only as a human being, but as a person with whom I share a special or unique relationship. I know that this person loves me, and that he or she would not intentionally say or do anything to harm me (thinkers know that cognitively and feelers sense it emotionally). If I hear this person say something which is not consistent with this belief, I need to check my perception or speak with him or her to ascertain where my lack of understanding has occurred. I am committed to this person in a special way, and I will treat him or her with love, respect, and gentleness. I will not allow any issue or misunderstanding to cause a deterioration in our communication. If we disagree (which is both inevitable and healthy), I will do so with a loving heart and an honest mind. To do otherwise would be to violate my commitment to this person whom I love." I would like to see a show of hands of all of us who repeat that consistently every time we enter into a conflict situation with someone we love.

Allow me to offer one more example, this time from the world of work. A professional colleague does not understand my position or stance on a particular issue, and is "clearly" guilty of benign ignorance. I circle the octagon (is that an oxymoron?), and I determine what course of action I must take, but I do so with this thought in mind: "I respect this person, not only as a human being, but as someone with whom I have a professional relationship. I know that this person has some special abilities or talents at the workplace, and is someone who is trying to succeed professionally, just as I am. I also realize that we will probably continue to work together, so it is in our best mutual interest to maintain a positive and healthy relationship. Although we may disagree at times, I will make a concentrated effort to indicate that my disagreement is not a personal issue, but a professional one. Furthermore, we disagree because we both care deeply about the issue in question. I will actively listen to the best of my ability, to really hear what he or she has to say. I will attempt to bring harmony to the relationship, even during the course of conflict and disagreement. Finally (here is the <u>real</u> test of commitment), I will strive to maintain the relationship, even if the other person fails to do the same. I will quietly, yet assertively, explain that I cannot communicate effectively unless there is mutual respect and adult-adult behavior. I will resist the temptation to fight fire with fire, which would prevent meaningful interaction in the future. To do otherwise would violate my commitment to be a professional employee." Do I dare ask for a show of hands on this one?

The elimination of the assumption of benign ignorance on the part of others is a colossal step toward un-tunneling our lives, and creating and maintaining significant relationships with the YOUs who are so precious to us. It is a giant leap toward relational maturity, in that it opens up brand new vistas, and it frees us from the restraining cords of "unconsciously assumed perfection" on our parts. I cannot overstate this point. If I relate to a YOU in my life with proactive understanding, acceptance, and desire to learn, I will catapult myself into a new stratosphere of relationship euphoria. The only thing holding me back is my refusal (or inability) to escape from the prison of my tunnel.

Summary of Part 2

As stated earlier, the chief objective of Part 1 of this book has been to allow all of us the opportunity to get to know ourselves better. Hopefully having accomplished that, the main objective of Part 2 has been to better understand the people who are most important to us. We have taken a close look at the YOUs in our world, to attempt to understand why they cannot be perfect like we are. We have grudgingly admitted that their differences are not severe or devious or insidious, but they are darned irritating when they get in the way of our perceptions, opinions, and judgments. We have labeled their differences "benign ignorance," because we know that they mean well, but they just don't understand. We have tolerated them because they are important people in our lives, but we have continued to be frustrated by their lack of perfection.

We have also taken a giant leap into the world of vulnerability by admitting the possibility that it is us who suffer from benign ignorance. We have made a valiant attempt to plant a STOP sign before us when we assume that our YOUs do not understand things as we do, and therefore are wrong. We have been open to measures such as: un-tunneling our vision, being sensitive, listening actively, using I-Statements, stating opinions instead of judgments, asking clarifying questions, looking for contrary perceptions, and committing ourselves to the relationship with our YOUs. If we have been successful in both our aptitudes and attitudes, then we are ready to explore the next step in our continuous quest toward creating successful relationships with all the people in our worlds.

PART 3

CHAPTER 7

◆◆◆

WHAT ARE FRIENDS FOR ANYWAY?

"What is a friend? A single soul
dwelling in two bodies"
– Aristotle
(quoted in _Familiar Quotations_, p. 97)

One of the most marvelous opportunities we have as human beings is the opportunity to become intimate with other people. We are fortuitous above other species in that we can relate on as deep a level as we choose. While animals are certainly capable of communicating with each other (probably in a far more sophisticated way than we imagine), few of us believe that they have the capacity for relating with each other in as complex and intricate a manner as do humans. We are truly blessed, and yet the vast majority of us do not even begin to penetrate the surface of our options for intimacy.

To some, intimacy conjures up visions of sexual involvement. That is certainly one form of intimacy, but it is only one expression of intimate feelings, appreciations, responses, caring, and loving. In fact, sexual intercourse is extremely limiting in its definition of intimacy in the eyes of many of us, as we typically confine that experience to include only one other person. But I choose to be intimate with several different people, of both genders, and so I must broaden my view of intimacy to include all that is important in a truly meaningful relationship. For example, I may have romantic intimacy with one person, but I also appreciate intimate relationships I have with close friends, both male and female.

The ancient Greeks had three words for love. **Agape** was the word used to express the love that God the Creator had for mankind. It assumed a kind of protectionist or "holy" love, one that a mother or father would have for their children. The second word, **philo**, was used to describe love for a close friend with whom one had an intimate relationship. Our English word, philanthropy, comes from this root. This described the deep feelings one might have for another, kind of a brother and sister type love. The third word, **eros**, indicated a romantic love, with sexual overtones. We get the word "erotic" from this. Unfortunately, in our modern day world, this concept has been diluted to mean anything that is sexually stimulating (pornography, X-rated videos, etc). The Greeks used the word to reflect a romantic type of love, not just one with sexual overtones. With apologies to those who enjoyed the movie "Pretty Woman," when was the last time you heard of a prostitute falling in love with her "John?"

It is unfortunate that we have only one word for love. We use synonyms such as: fond of, like a lot (as opposed to just like), care for, have feelings for, really like a lot, etc. Sometimes we avoid the "L" word because it might be misinterpreted (when I was about 10 years old, my parents were aghast when I wrote to my grandparents, and signed the letter, "Sincerely, Bill"). Even though I loved them dearly, I felt foolish putting it in writing. I wish I could have written, "Love (grandparental love, not God love or friendly love or sexual love, just grandparental love), Bill."

If we can agree with the concepts described above, then it seems only natural that we define our intimate relationships as those we experience with "special" YOUs in our lives. Here we need to make a differentiation between YOUs and special YOUs. While I have numerous YOUs in my life, there are relatively few with whom I desire intimacy in one form or another. I may consider a co-worker a YOU because I care about the person, and interact with him or her on a daily basis, but I also may choose not to share significant parts of my life with that individual (intimacy). He or she is a vocational YOU, not an intimate YOU.

For the purposes of the rest of Part 3 of this book, make a list of those people in your life with whom you believe you share some degree of intimacy, a special relationship that is deeply important to you. If it helps, put these in categories, such as:

- spouse, or significant other
- family members
- close personal friends

Keep in mind that this is not necessarily a hierarchy, just a system to determine how I express my love and intimacy to these special people. For example, it is natural for me to verbally express love to my spouse or significant other, and to be quite physical about it. With my children, the verbal expression must also be frequent, but the physical expression will be appropriately different. When it comes to close personal friends, both the verbal and physical expressions of love will be less frequent, although the communication between us should be reinforcing of our special relationship.

When I stated that this is not necessarily a hierarchy, what I meant was that one does not always have to be <u>most</u> intimate with a spouse, <u>next</u> with family members, and <u>lastly</u> with close friends. Ideally, one should be maximally intimate with all three, although in different contexts, styles, and intensities. Let me provide you with a hypothetical example. Todd is married, has three children, and is extremely close friends with two of his co-workers (one male and one female). There are certain areas of Todd's life that he shares with his wife, and with no one else. If you were to ask Todd if he considers his wife his "best friend," he might reply, "Yes she is my best friend. But my children are also my best friends, and two people at work are also my best friends. I have several best friends, depending on what kind of relationship you are talking about." Therefore, there may be certain areas of Todd's life that he shares with his children, even more than with his wife. There may also be some significant intimacy that he shares with his friends at work only. It is not that he has anything to hide from his family, but some things might be better understood, accepted, and responded to by close friends who see Todd in a different light. The different relationships are not better or worse, nor are they necessarily mutually exclusive, but they provide for a wholistic framework for Todd, as he attempts to achieve intimacy with the most significant YOUs in his life.

Let me digress for a moment here to quickly add that there may be some areas of one's life that he or she chooses not to share with <u>anyone</u>. In other words, intimacy with self on occasions is not weird, unhealthy, or a sign of paranoia. At times, intimacy may be so precious and personal that to divulge it to others (even the most sacred of relationships) would be to violate an inner peace or privilege. There is a very interesting verse in chapter two of the book of Luke in *The Bible*. The story is about the birth of Jesus, and how the shepherds followed the star to Bethlehem to see the new-born baby. The author expounds on the exuberance of the shepherds, stating that they announced to people far and wide that an angel had told them that this child was the Savior sent from God. After they spread the news, they returned, "glorifying and praising God." And yet in the middle of all this celebration and pronouncement, there is a verse tucked away that reads, "But Mary (the mother of Jesus) kept all these things, and pondered them in her heart." It would indicate that the experience was of such personal and significant meaning to her, that she chose not to share it with anyone, including her husband. She preferred to reflect in the quietness of her own heart and soul the meaning of that event in her life.

Have you ever had moments like that? I have, and I make no apology for keeping them to myself. Does that mean I don't love or trust others with whom I share intimacy? No, of course not. It just means there are thoughts for which I have no words that others will understand, or I flash-back to events in my life that are so privately intense and meaningful that I choose to maintain self-intimacy.

Now let's return to the subject at hand—those people with whom we are intimate. What I want to concentrate on in the next couple of chapters is how we build and maintain closer relationships with those special people in our lives, and how we handle the intricate components of those relationships, such as communication, confrontation, and conflict. Part 1 of this book was titled "ME" because it was introspective. Part 2 was titled "YOU" because we looked outward to others who are significant in our lives. Part 3 is titled "US" because it examines relationships. No longer are we ME and YOU, but we are US. We are one in the relationship, and here we want to investigate life within that union. Every coach in the history of sports has told his or her team, "There is no I in TEAM." There is no room for selfishness or egocentrism. Without the relationship, there is no team. The same is true here. Concentrate on your intimate relationships as US. Only then will this part of the book make sense.

Three Relationships

It might be helpful for you to engage in an exercise at this point. Identify three people with whom you are intimate in one capacity or another, preferably three different <u>kinds</u> of intimate people; a spouse or significant other (if you have one), a family member with whom you feel particularly close, and a very good friend. Complete the three statements below and, without sharing your responses, have the three intimate people also complete the statements. Note the similarities and differences, and then share the responses.

1. The five things that make our relationship very special are

2. Of all the things I value about our relationship, the one ingredient I <u>most</u> treasure is

3. If we could improve the relationship between us in <u>one</u> significant way, it would be

I am willing to go out on a limb at this point, and suggest that the responses from you and your intimate friends included some or all of the relationship ingredients I am about to mention. There are numerous elements we could factor in, but those could fill another entire book. For now, let me suggest **four actions which I consider** critical in order to establish and maintain a quality intimate relationship, whether it be romantic, familial, or social/occupational.

Look at the graph on the following page, featuring the four actions. Each one is perceived a certain way, has an antagonist which prevents its effectiveness at maintaining the relationship, and has a remedy which can preserve the relationship. In my opinion, they are equal in importance and value, and some rely on the existence of the others in order to be effective. I believe all four actions must be present in order to maintain and grow an intimate relationship.

When you were in school, the letter "F" was something to be avoided like the plague—in fact, if I recall correctly from my own experience, it <u>was</u> a plague of some proportion. But here, the letter "F" is a good thing, and something to be desired and cherished. I would suggest that if we consistently practice the four Fs, our relationships will be meaningful, intensely important, and growing. Accordingly, I have worded them as action verbs because they require constant attention and hard work.

ACTION	BE FEELING	BE FUELING	BE FEEDING	BE FORTHRIGHT
PERCEPTION	SENSITIVITY	SUPPPORT	STIMULATION	SINCERITY
ANTAGONIST	TUNNEL VISION	TEDIUM BUILD-UP	TRANSCENDENCE INHIBITION	TRUST DEPRIVATION
REMEDY	COMMITMENT	COMMITMENT	COMMITMENT	COMMITMENT

BE FEELING

This is perceived as sensitivity. For some of us, it comes naturally, while for others of us, we have to work real hard at it. Basically, it means always being aware of how our "other half" of the relationship is doing—physically, mentally, emotionally, psychologically. It means being aware of the subtle cues which he or she is giving out, cues which indicate that everything is all right, or not all right. It means reading between the lines of what is said, or the responses to what we have said. It means caring for the person in such a way that we hear not only words, but inner thoughts and feelings, hurts and wants, unspoken requests and pleas. It means entering into every facet of the conversation or encounter with an attempt to put the other person's needs above my own, to listen more than talk, to catch the excitement or enthusiasm which he or she is trying to share, or to equally feel the anguish or hurt which he or she is experiencing. This is tough work, and it is one of the reasons why most of us cannot handle very many close YOUs in our lives. In most cases, we are either incapable of feeling at the deepest levels, or we really just don't care enough to do it because it is such an exhausting experience. It needs to be reserved for our most intimate YOUs.

Let's return for a minute to temperament types. It would be easy to say that feelers are naturally good at this, and that thinkers are not, and therefore, they need to work harder in order to be feeling people. For feelers it is a breeze, and for thinkers it is a formidable task. I personally don't agree with that, for two reasons.

First, if you recall, feelers can be both compassionate and vindictive. For compassionate feelers, this is indeed a natural activity. They tend to live in a relationship world, and they typically assume the best about others. They are usually adept at understanding where others are coming from (especially if they are intuitors), and they have a natural tendency to be accepting and understanding. But vindictive feelers are another story. They do not necessarily assume the best about others, and in fact, they may be the last people to understand where others are coming from because emotionally they do not agree with or understand the other's point of view. In my opinion, vindictive feelers are even less able than most thinkers to be sensitive in a relationship when things go awry.

Second, and related to the first reason, there tends to be a misconception regarding thinkers, which we have discussed earlier in this book. Thinkers are not necessarily cold, hard, cruel tyrants, although they can be. Thinkers just tend to use logic and rational thought instead of emotions when they view situations. Thinkers can be consummate "feeling" people, although they do so from a perspective which is different from feelers. For example, a thinker may be incredibly sensitive to a YOU in his or her life because it is the right way to demonstrate love, affection, or friendship. This person may not say, "I will be extremely sensitive because it is how I want to be treated," but he or she may say, "I know that this is the appropriate manner in which to display my sincere sensitivity." It may sound paradoxical, but in some cases, thinkers may be more capable of "feeling" than feelers.

The antagonist to feeling is tunnel vision, as we have discussed in previous chapters. It is the inability or unwillingness to view situations from the perspective of another. In the case of inability, I need to recognize that it is not my natural tendency, and both concentration and conscious effort are necessary in order to take the next step. In the case of unwillingness, I need to recognize that my ego or pride or stubbornness are in the way, and must be overcome by a strong desire to maintain the relationship.

The remedy for tunnel vision, as a detriment to feeling, is commitment—commitment to the relationship in terms of my own sensitivity to the other person involved. Without true commitment, I will either refuse to make the sacrificial effort to improve the relationship, or I will stage a good outward show, while harboring my own feelings of hurt or martyrdom. In either case, the results will be short-lived, at best, and the relationship will not be mutually satisfactory over the long haul.

It is a sham to refer to an acquaintance as an "intimate relationship" if the individuals are not being feeling to each other. I personally have never known two people to have a positive, healthy relationship where one of them felt the other was insensitive and unfeeling. Think about the relationships in your life which you consider intimate (romantic, familial, social/occupational). What is your feeling quotient? Was that a factor in the three-statement survey you gave to your intimate YOUs?

BE FUELING

This is perceived as support. When I was in college, I learned a very painful lesson. This is not profound, and you probably do not need to be sitting down to absorb the impact, but here is the lesson I learned: when a car runs out of gas, it stops moving. You can talk to it, swear at it, and kick it, but nothing will alter the end result. No gas, no go!

The same is true with intimate relationships. If there is no constant infusing of fuel, the thing will die. Bear with me while I carry the automobile analogy a step further. The car may have exquisite leather upholstering, new tires, bucket seats, computerized dashboard, fresh paint, etc., but if there is no fuel in the tank, it becomes a statue. It is nice to look at, but it gets you nowhere. Let me say that again. It is nice to look at, but it gets you nowhere.

Do you have any "intimate relationships" like that? All the pretty pieces are in place, but it is going nowhere. There is money in the bank, furniture in all the rooms, cooperation on projects, time (possibly grudgingly) spent with the kids or friends, and sincere effort spent on keeping things on an even keel. But where is the fuel? Where is the support?

> *"The lights are on, but nobody's home."*
> *– Anonymous*

Let me offer a well-publicized antagonist which drains the gas tank. It is called tedium build-up. Maybe the relationship has existed for so long that ennui has occurred. The spark has vanished. The embers are hardly warm. The faults you never saw before now carry neon lights. It is not that you want to terminate the relationship—it is just that it isn't as consuming as it once was. Other interests now occupy the front burner, and absorb the fresh energy and passion. And interestingly, this does not occur exclusively with romantic relationships. It can happen between parents and children, where all the reasoning, explaining, cajoling, coaching, etc. have been ineffective, and now both parent and child have resigned themselves to a flat relationship. It can happen between friends or co-workers, but on a different level. What used to excite you as Mary's creativity, you now label instability, and you tire of her ever-changing ideas. What once thrilled you as Tom's consistency, you now consider boring and un-adventurous. The doting and TLC you once craved from Lucy now "smothers" you. In turn, you withdraw from fueling, and the rest is fairly predictable. Sounds gloomy, doesn't it? So what can I do to keep fueling my relationship, other than to fake it?

The remedy for tedium build-up is commitment—commitment to the relationship in terms of not being willing to allow it to fade because of the passage of time, or because of current interests or exciting novelties. I would closely examine the relationship to determine if it is worth keeping, and if so, take the following steps to preserve it. First, I would suggest confronting head-on the reasons for why the tedium build-up has embedded itself in my psyche. My guess is that it did not happen overnight, nor because of one single incident or comment. We all tend to grow impatient or dissatisfied over time with status quo situations, and it would be most helpful to study why that has occurred. Has it been a conscious trend (possibly the introduction of a new idea or opportunity or friend), or an unconscious drifting? In either case, an honest appraisal of the tedium build-up is a necessary first step.

Second, I would suggest questioning why the tedium build-up has not been addressed before now. Perhaps it is because unconsciously I have not paid attention to the relationship in recent times. Or perhaps it is because I have subconsciously allowed the relationship to falter, in order to gather momentum for ending it, or because I believe the other person should have addressed the issue with me (I have hurt feelings, and I have been taken advantage of). Once again, I need to understand where my feelings and intentions are in this dilemma.

Last, I would suggest thinking of ways to terminate either the tedium build-up or the relationship. Like any other organism, including the body, if a relationship is not growing, it will atrophy. Middle ground lasts only so long—after that, there is either life or death. The death may be swift, or it may be painfully slow, but death is the result, and people get hurt. Whether the relationship is romantic, familial, or social/occupational, in order to remain a true intimate relationship, fueling must take place. So what is your fueling quotient? Was that a factor in the three-statement survey you gave to your intimate YOUs?

BE FEEDING

This is perceived as stimulation. At first blush, it may be easy to confuse with fueling, but it is a more active step. It goes beyond merely supporting another person (in the past and present sense), and it concentrates on strengthening the other (in the future sense). In that regard, it is growth oriented. It assumes that the fueling support is present on a consistent basis. Feeding not only provides petrol for the car, but also equips it with an engine, good tires, fun ideas of where to travel, and a road map showing how to get there. Feeding is concentrating on such things as potential, opportunity, and growth.

If Sarah supports Daniel in his quest to find a better job, or quit smoking, or act more positively toward his associates and co-workers, she is fueling him. If she provides the moral and spiritual assistance he needs, and lends advice when he requests it, she is pouring gasoline into his tank. But if Sarah goes beyond the support stage, and actually seeks out opportunities and possibilities for Daniel, then she is feeding him. Perhaps she identifies an area of her life with which she is dissatisfied, such as procrastination. She approaches Daniel and offers, "Let's make a pact and hold each other accountable. I will assist you in your efforts to stop smoking, and you assist me in my efforts to stop procrastinating. Let's find a way to make it fun and profitable for both of us."

"Procrastinate later."
– Anonymous

That is feeding because it goes beyond support, and attempts to stimulate, strengthen, and promote growth. Then let's imagine that Daniel encourages Sarah to return to school to pursue her long-time ambition of becoming a nurse. He suggests ways that it might be affordable, and he offers to share some of her current responsibilities in order to allow her time for study and class attendance. That is feeding because it demonstrates excitement in assisting the intimate relationship partner to pursue her potential.

I encountered a situation similar to this just recently. A co-worker, who happens to be one of my most intimate YOUs, had assumed extra responsibility at work. After a number of months, he became increasingly irritable, crabby, and difficult to be with. We had lunch, and I offered to take on the extra responsibility myself (even though I desperately did not want the additional work load) because, as I put it, "This is driving you crazy, and you are driving me crazy, and I would rather put up with extra responsibility than see you miserable and jeopardize our special relationship." This was not a heroic act on my part. It is the type of feeding that anyone with a treasured intimate relationship would provide, as he has for me on numerous occasions.

The other day, I was contemplating this concept of the intimate relationship, and I strolled to the window of my office. In a tree, not more than 15 yards from my window, was a mother bird feeding a worm to her two babies. It hit me like a ton of bricks—feeding each other is intimacy. In some relationships, the feeding is appropriately uni-dimensional, as with a mother and a baby. In most meaningful relationships, however, the feeding is a two-way street. We actively and consciously seek ways to assist our relationship partner in growth experiences.

The antagonist here is what I term transcendence inhibition. Perhaps we are envious of another's ambition, and so seek ways to thwart the effort. Perhaps our egos are so fragile that we cannot allow another to thrive and feel fulfilled. In my role as an adult educator, I have encountered literally dozens of cases where a woman wishes to return to school in order to complete her undergraduate degree, but her husband attempts to squash the dream. In many cases, it was she who worked to put him through school, but he has no desire to witness her achievement at the same level. He feels much better about himself knowing that he has a higher degree, a better paying job, and a more exciting life-style. Attempting to inhibit the transcendence effort of my "intimate relationship partner" is an unmistakable billboard advertisement of my selfish facade at true relationship.

The remedy for transcendence inhibition is commitment—commitment to the relationship in terms of my desire to help my relationship partner experience all that he or she can toward growth, satisfaction, achievement, and reaching fulfillment through the process of "becoming." Once again, I need to ask myself if I am really committed to this particular relationship. If not, then a sure way of demonstrating that is to play one-upsmanship, inhibit transcendence toward growth, and attempt to keep the person at a level of subservience. But if I am truly committed to the person as an intimate relationship partner, then I will seek ways to encourage him or her toward growth opportunities. I will exercise sensitivity in recognizing those growth opportunities (Be Feeling), support in not allowing tedium build-up to occur (Be Fueling), and stimulation in creatively finding ways to make those growth opportunities a reality (Be Feeding). So what is your feeding quotient? Was that a factor in the three-statement survey you gave to your intimate YOUs?

<u>BE FORTHRIGHT</u>

This is perceived as sincerity. It is the glue which holds all the other pieces in place. Without forthrightness, or intentional honesty, not much else can be counted on in a relationship. In study after study, over many years, where people have been asked to identify the most important characteristics of their spouses, friends, bosses, ministers, politicians, school teachers, and other significant individuals in their lives, one of the top two or three responses has been "integrity" or "honesty." There is something about human nature which craves honesty from others, although most of us would admit that we are not always honest with those others. Many of us would shout, "Just tell me the truth. I can handle it," although we choose to sometimes not tell the truth because we feel that <u>they</u> cannot handle it.

That seems rather strange to me. In a scene from the movie, "A Few Good Men," Colonel Nathan Jessup (played by Jack Nicholsen) is on the witness stand, responding to questions from the prosecuting attorney, Lieutenant Dan Caffey (played by Tom Cruise) regarding the hazing death of a marine. As the verbal confrontation becomes more heated, Cruise demands that Nicholsen tell the truth, and Nicholsen screams, "You can't handle the truth!" Somehow we feel that we are impervious, and therefore deserve truth at all times, but that others are weak, and must be sheltered from reality.

Of course, that is only one reason for being less than forthright. Another, and probably more common, is that we have something to hide. At this point, let's keep in mind that we are concentrating on the intimate relationship partners in our lives. This means that we can dispense with the everyday encounters we have with non-intimate relationship partners, such as, "The check is in the mail," or "I never received that memo," or "No, she is not in right now—may I take a message?" I want to concentrate on intentional honesty with our intimate relationship partners.

> *"Candor is a compliment; it implies equality.*
> *It's how true friends talk."*
> *– Peggy Noonan*
> *(quoted in Quotable Quotes, p. 122)*

Have you ever been in a relationship where the other person was honest with you 99% of the time? What did you think about that percentage? Was it good enough? On a math test, it would be almost an A+. As a batting average, it would be about three times what the best hitters achieve. In an election, it would give unprecedented meaning to the term "landslide." But in an intimate relationship, 99% honesty gives cause for doubt, concern, suspicion, and fear. Anything less than 100% raises questions about the intimacy of the relationship. Talk about raising the bar! It is perfection, or it is nothing, and that is serious business.

The logical question now follows: if one is in an intimate relationship, why would that person even think about being less than forthright? I would suggest that there is only one reason (assuming the relationship is truly mutually intimate), but it can be applied to both of the scenarios mentioned above. This is the antagonist, which I call trust deprivation. The key question is, "How will he or she react if I tell the truth?" and the two scenarios are: how will he or she react if I have something to hide (guilty), and how will he or she react if I need to share something (innocent) which might not be well received?

I remember as a child that I was afraid to lie to my parents. The reason for this was that if I did something wrong, I would be punished, but if I lied about it, I would die an excruciatingly painful death. As a result, I did not lie very often, but I chose my battles carefully. I only lied when I was so afraid that the reaction to my misdemeanor would be as severe as the reaction to my lying, and therefore, it was worth the gamble. For the most part, I have continued that behavior throughout my life. I am not terribly proud of it, but on occasions I have reasoned that telling the truth might not be worth the consequences. Let me illustrate the two scenarios mentioned above.

Chuck and Ed are co-workers, and best of friends for many years. They confide in each other, would do anything for each other, and interact as frequently as they can. One day, Chuck accidentally mentions something to another co-worker which he promised Ed he would never reveal.

He immediately realizes his error, and begs the other co-worker not to breathe a word to anyone else, as his reputation with Ed would be on the line. The co-worker pledges to keep it a secret (and we all know that a secret is something you tell only one person at a time). Eventually the word gets back to Ed, and he asks Chuck, in a most pathetically betrayed voice, "Did you mention that to anyone?"

Now Chuck has a decision to make. Should he confess, apologize, and hope that Ed understands that the error was not intentional, or should he emphatically declare that he would never betray his friend, in order not to risk the relationship? Have you ever been there? I have, and it makes you think real hard about the strength of the relationship. If Chuck admits his mistake, will Ed understand? Will he forgive? More importantly, will he forget? Will the relationship ever be the same again, or will there remain the faint doubt that Chuck is totally trustworthy?

Let's look at the second scenario. Marcie and Fran have been friends since childhood. Now they are approaching 40 and realizing that they may be nearing the half-way point of life. Fran is married, and has a family and a full-time job, which she enjoys. She is quite satisfied with her life. In her mind, she has the best of all worlds. Marcie has never been married, but often has mentioned that she would like to be in a family situation similar to Fran's. She has a good career, but she has experienced several disappointing dating situations in recent years. She understands that she is not as attractive to strangers as she once was, and she also realizes that the men she knows are already married or "just friends." She down-plays her loneliness with Fran, but continues to express her desire to be in a comfortable relationship with a caring man.

Lately, Marcie has altered her wardrobe, opting for shorter skirts and tighter-fitting sweaters. She has dated several men, each considerably younger than she is. She has been openly flirtatious with some of the married men at work. Fran, of course, has noticed Marcie's apparel and behavior, and is quite concerned about her life-long friend. At one point, she jokingly alluded to Marcie's knack for drawing male attention, but Marcie reacted angrily, stating that she was not interested in leering men. Fran is now concerned that Marcie may be on the verge of making some mistakes which could ruin her life, and some other people's marriages. She desperately wants to speak with Marcie about what she is going through, but she is afraid of what the reaction will be. She loves her friend dearly, and does not want to do anything which could jeopardize their relationship. So what does she do? Does she take the risk, and lovingly confront her friend? Does she bide her time, hoping that the "new" Marcie is only a passing fad? How does she demonstrate her intentional honesty and forthrightness with her intimate relationship partner in such a way so as to strengthen the relationship?

The remedy for trust deprivation is commitment (do you sense a pattern here?)—commitment to the relationship in terms of being forthright with the intimate partner because nothing less will do, and yet being loving and caring to the point that the truth does not come crashing down like a sledge-hammer, but rather delicately surrounds the intimate partner as a caressing hug. So what is your forthright quotient? Was that a factor in the three-statement survey you gave to your intimate YOUs?

I mentioned in a previous chapter that one of the most profound expressions I have ever heard comes from _The Bible_, and goes like this: "Speak the truth in love." Reflect on that as you turn to the next chapter.

CHAPTER 8

◆◆◆

I'LL BE HONEST WITH YOU

"Speak The Truth In Love"
The Bible

Seldom have I seen more powerful words than those written above. In fact, if I were asked to sum up the total concept of communication in one sentence, I would quote, "Speak the truth in love." Unfortunately, effective communication is not quite that simple, but I can't think of a better way to begin. Most of us fail to understand the balance required to speak the truth in love. We tend to be too far to either extreme of the spectrum to truly grasp how profound the statement is, and as a result, we emphasize one at the expense of the other.

Many of us have a tendency to be truthful, perhaps blatantly so, because truth is all-important, but we lack the skills or attitude to express that truth in loving ways. And truth without love is barbarian. Others of us have a tendency to be loving or soothing because we feel that tenderness is at the root of relationship maintenance, but we lack the skills or understanding to express that love in truthful ways. And love without truth is pabulum. Even if we don't express it verbally, some of us think that we must tell the truth, <u>but</u> do it lovingly. Others of us think that we must be loving, <u>but</u> tell the truth. I would suggest that a mature understanding of this concept substitutes the word "therefore" for the word "but." I love this intimate relationship partner, therefore I will tell the truth. I am truthful with this intimate relationship partner, therefore I will do it lovingly. If the two do not go hand-in-hand, there is discord, misunderstanding, hurt, and damaged relationships. If they do go hand-in-hand, there is harmony, admiration, love, and growth.

Because so much of this book deals with communication, it seems almost redundant to devote an entire chapter to it at this point.

Therefore, I would like to focus very specifically on three facets of communication between intimate relationship partners:

1. truth telling
2. conflict resolution
3. intentional listening

These three communication imperatives could be (and have been) topics for entire books on each one. My purpose here is not to lay out complicated philosophies or impressive formulas, nor to repeat what we have read in former chapters. Rather, I would like to speak directly from my heart about some down-to-earth practical ideas which might be helpful for us to consider as we attempt to improve our communication with those whom we love the most.

In 20 years of teaching adult students, I have had hundreds of them confirm to me that the most difficult problem they encounter in meaningful relationships is the inability to communicate effectively on a regular basis. Most of them are quick to blame the other person in the relationship (spouse, friend, family member, co-worker), and so we spend considerable time going through exercises like you have seen in previous chapters of this book. This assists us in understanding that the communication is a two-way street, and that we are typically just as guilty as the other person when it comes to having tunnel vision, assuming benign ignorance, and not really trying to understand. If you presume that you also might tend to automatically blame your intimate partner for communication breakdowns, pause here for a moment, and return to the STOP sign in chapter six.

Try to isolate which of the points on the octagon is your nemesis. Maybe you have two or three of them. Identify them. Write them down. Memorize them. Make it a conscious effort on your part to be aware of them when you are communicating. Above all, keep this in mind: I will never be able to communicate effectively as long as I tend to blame all the communication snafus on the other person. If I am looking for a scapegoat, I am not looking for improvement in the communication. I need to be sure that my focus is on my efforts to communicate effectively, not on the barriers which might be in the way.

Imagine you are a high hurdler at a track meet. As you stand at the starting line, you look ahead on the track and think, "I'll never get to the finish line because there are so many darned hurdles in my way." Isn't that a strange thought? And at the end of the race, when you do not finish as well as you would have liked to, you think, "I would have done well if it had not been for those hurdles in my way." Effective communication is like that. It is never an easy task, especially over many months or years. There are always hurdles in the lane that must be overcome. And if we choose to focus on the hurdles, and blame them for our lack of success, then we will continue to have a lack of success. We will feel slightly better about the fact that we have something to blame it on, but we will not achieve the goal of effective communication.

It is only when I own up to the fact that I am equally responsible for past failures, and future attempts, at effective communication that it will actually become a reality. One of my students once submitted a paper which contained the following: "One thing that was apparent to me as I compared the satisfied workers with the dissatisfied workers was that the onus of responsibility for our professional lives does not fall solely on the backs of our supervisors. . . we need to take responsibility to improve some areas of our lives. Many of the reasons listed above had to do with interpersonal qualities, which we all have some control over as we function in our daily teams." I would submit that the same is true of communication patterns.

Let's look at the three imperatives for effective communication between intimate relationship partners.

Imperative I
Truth Telling

In chapter seven, we referred to this as BE FORTHRIGHT. I suggested that there is one basic reason (trust deprivation) why intimate people might be less than truthful with each other, but it can easily take two forms. The overarching reason is that we are afraid how the other person will respond, and the two forms are: I have something to hide (guilty) or I don't want this person to be hurt (innocent). Wouldn't it be nice if all of our relationships were of such caliber that we could be totally truthful in any circumstance? Of course, that takes the innocence of a child, but even that child soon learns that being intentionally honest is not always in his or her best interest.

I still get tears in my eyes when I recall this experience. When my twin sons were very young, probably about two years old, Matthew discovered that his teeth were not only made for chewing food, but could be used as effective weapons against his brother during a dispute. The first time this happened when I was home, Michael let out a blood-curdling scream and showed me his arm, which had serious teeth marks etched in it. I asked Matthew, "Did you bite Michael?" (Upon reflection, I realize that was a rather stupid question, but at the time it seemed appropriate). Matthew looked at me with his beautiful blue eyes, and innocently said, "Yes." I then told him how naughty it was to bite, and I swatted him on his rear end. He of course cried, so I held him (crying along with him because it broke my heart to have to spank him) and told him that I loved him, but that he could not bite his brother.

It happened a second time, with the same results—he admitted it and received a spanking. Several days later, the incident occurred again, and I asked the same dumb question, "Did you bite Michael?" But this time the response was different. He looked at me with pleading eyes and said, "Don't hit me." So I had taught my son to equate truth telling with punishment. He quickly learned that if he wished to avoid pain, it was in his best interest not to admit to a wrong-doing.

How different was that two-year-old boy from you and me today? How often do we skirt around the truth with significant people in our lives so that we do not have to endure punishment of one kind or another (hurt feelings, angry looks or comments, silence, isolation)? Does it have to be that way, or is it really possible to be intentionally honest with our intimate partners at all times, no matter what? I think the answer to that lies in the strength of the relationship, and in the ability to both give and receive the truth in love, and that is one of the tallest orders I have ever heard of.

> *The genius of communication is the ability to be both totally honest and totally kind at the same time."*
> *– John Powell*
> (quoted in <u>Quotable Quotes,</u> p. 122)

In the final few pages of the last chapter, I gave two scenarios regarding truth telling. In the first, Chuck inadvertently betrayed a friend's secret. He did not do it maliciously, and he felt terrible about it immediately afterward. When his friend Ed asked him about the incident, Chuck had to decide how he would respond. Would he be honest, and risk the consequences of a broken relationship, or would he lie to preserve the friendship? Ideally, Chuck would confess his indiscretion, explain that it was an innocent (although terrible) mistake, and ask Ed to forgive him. Ideally, Ed would forgive, stating that he understood and trusted his friend. Ideally, everyone would live happily ever after. Unfortunately, those old-time television relational partners Ozzie and Harriet, the Cleavers, and the Honeymooners do not live on every street in every town, and reality can be devastatingly awful.

The other scenario featured Marcie and Fran, and Fran's dilemma of whether or not to express to Marcie her concerns about Marcie's current lifestyle. Does Fran tell the truth to her friend in a loving way, and risk a relational split, or does she keep her ideas to herself to preserve the peace, but allow Marcie to enter dangerously thin ice without caring counsel? Ideally, Fran would approach Marcie, assure her of her love, and convince her that her concern is a reflection of that love. Ideally, Marcie would welcome the concern and care from a close friend, and listen to her sage advice. But it doesn't always work that way, and truth telling can be a huge risk-taking proposition.

Let me mention something I have observed regarding truth telling and temperament types. Thinkers are more apt to tell the truth, and to want to be told the truth, whereas feelers are more apt to want to be spared the truth if it is not good news, and to withhold the truth if it might produce uncomfortable results. That is not always the case, of course, but it is a tendency. Let me illustrate with a rather inconsequential example.

A number of years ago, I used the word "appraise" in a memo to a student when I should have used the word "apprise." A colleague who read the memo pointed out the mistake to me. As a thinker, I immediately thanked the colleague, was grateful for the correction, and have never made the same mistake again. On the other hand, I have several very close friends who are feelers, and they absolutely detest being corrected on minor issues such as word choice, etc. It took me a while, but I have learned not to introduce corrections with them, although it is my natural tendency to do so. Since thinkers do not internalize the same way feelers do, thinkers view some areas of truth telling more objectively, while feelers view those same areas more subjectively. To many feelers, being corrected is somewhat humiliating (parent-child interaction), and while thinkers do not perceive it that way, or mean to imply it that way, they need to be aware of the feelers' sensitivities.

Take that concept one step further. What if a significant person in your life says to you, "I just bought this new dress (or shirt or blouse or tie). Do you like it?" You might want to gear your response in a way that would fit with his or her temperament. With a thinker, you could probably say, "Not really. I don't think it is "you." With a feeler, you might want to say something like, "I personally do not like that color or pattern, but if you like it, that is all that really matters. Not everybody will like the same things." What you are doing is telling the truth ("I personally do not like it"), but sparing the feelings. How we word our comments is crucial in any communication scenario.

In a perfect world, all intentional honesty would be offered and accepted in such a way so as to strengthen every relationship. But let me break the news gently, and I hope you're sitting down for this: we do not live in a perfect world. Nor do we live in perfect relationships. Most of us are fragile, insecure, and needy, and we have to work very hard at all times to maintain positive communication patterns and desirable relationships. Think back to my comment of a few pages ago in this chapter. I asked if it is really possible to be intentionally honest with our intimate partners at all times, no matter what, and I suggested that the answer to that lies in the strength of the relationship, and in the ability to both give and receive the truth in love. Let me stress that again. The strength of the relationship is the bottom line. I would like to believe that my most intimate relationships are so strong that I can say, "I will be lovingly honest with this person because he or she knows the depth of my love and commitment, and knows that I would never intentionally hurt him or her. If there is misunderstanding in our communication, we will be able to resolve the issue because we are committed to the relationship." And the corollary statement is, "I will accept without defensiveness or suspicion the loving truth telling of this person because I know that he or she loves me and is committed to our relationship. I know this person would never intentionally hurt me. If I misunderstand what he or she tells me, we will resolve the issue because we are both committed to the relationship."

In closing this section, allow me to ask one question. As you think about your most intimate relationships, do your reactions to truth telling communication discourage your partner from being intentionally honest with you? Do you state overtly, or imply covertly, that you prefer not to be told the truth? What signals do you tend to give that would communicate to your relational partners that you desire loving truth, or coded messages? Since we all suffer from the dreaded and ubiquitous tunnel vision, you might want to discuss this with those partners. Perhaps we are blind to some of the clues we emit, and it might be a good and profitable idea for us to have them exposed and explained to us. Truth telling is essential for effective perpetual communication between intimate relationship partners.

Imperative 2
Conflict Resolution

For most of my life, I have been told that nothing is as certain as death and taxes. I have no dispute with either of those inevitable eventualities, but I wish to add another equally unwelcome interloper—conflict. While it is not typically as economically depressing as paying taxes, nor as final as death, conflict is as natural and inescapable as either, and occurs with a great deal more frequency. The good news is that if we choose to do so, we have considerably more control over the conflict in our lives than we do over what Uncle Sam or the Grim Reaper require of us. That is the key to conflict resolution—we have control and we have choice.

As I stated at the outset of this chapter, the three communication imperatives of truth telling, conflict resolution, and intentional listening are so vast in concept that many volumes have been written about each one. I do not wish to reinvent the wheel nor cover the entire gamut of conflict resolution, but rather share a few brief ideas which I have found to be helpful in my life and relationships, and which may also be of encouragement and assistance to you. Please remember that they will be helpful only if they are blended with the other components of relational communication which we are discussing, such as the STOP sign concepts, truth telling, and intentional listening.

First, I would like to refute something which most of us have been taught all of our lives, and that is that conflict is bad, and always something to be avoided or repressed. I used to think that, but I no longer do. It is not conflict per se which is negative, but rather the misuse of conflict. In fact, I will go out on a limb and suggest that conflict can have tremendous benefits in terms of growing and being productive if it is managed lovingly and maturely. With apologies to Duke Ellington, let's take a quick ride on the A-Train to enumerate the benefits of conflict.

Attitude: conflict demonstrates that we care, that we are emotionally involved in the issue at hand. Without concern or involvement, there would be no conflict, but there would also be no attachment to critical areas of our lives.

Amplification: conflict helps to open the mind, to hear other perspectives, to rid us of the dreaded tunnel vision which most of us carry around with us like the weight of the world. Without conflict, we would be content with our own limited horizons, and be unaware of the expansion possibilities.

Alteration: conflict serves to assist us in changing our perceptions regarding those whose personalities and temperaments are different from our own. Without conflict, we would be prone to forget that those imperfect YOUs in our lives are not as weird as we once suspected, and that they actually have a legitimate place in the world.

Authorship: conflict is necessary for brainstorming, and for the creation of new ideas. Without conflict, we tend to gravitate toward the familiar and comfortable, and to shy away from the controversial potentials, thus limiting our scope.

Achievement: conflict helps us to go beyond authorship of ideas to creative approaches of decision-making and problem-solving. Without conflict, many good ideas would lie dormant on the drawing board and never come to fruition.

The story is told that Henry Ford once presented his inner circle of directors with a proposal, and asked for their reactions. Not wishing to confront the boss, no one voiced any objection, but rather nodded in silent agreement with the plan. Ford then adjourned the meeting, instructing his directors to return the next day with well-thought-out arguments and counter-proposals. He wanted to elicit caring conflict, not passive acquiescence, thereby creating a better product.

If we can agree that conflict is not always bad, but can produce some amazingly positive results, then the next step is to recognize the major causes of conflict, especially in its most negative context. Since we are dealing only with our most intimate relational partners here, let me limit the causes to four which I observe on a regular basis. I am not including here tunnel vision or closed-mindedness, which we have discussed at length previously. The quartet of culprits would be: ego, assumptions, expectations, and anxiety. Very quickly, let's examine these viruses.

Ego—need I say more? Have you ever had a confrontation encounter with a significant person in your life where you allowed ego to get in the way of productive resolution? Of course you haven't, but if you had, it would probably be because most of us regard conflict as win-lose, and we do not like to lose. As the conflict becomes apparent, the stubborn self will take center stage, the stance becomes entrenched, the positions become polarized, and the conflict becomes not only negative, but nasty. A conflict which began as incidental results in hurtful comments and innuendoes which cause damage to the relationship.

Assumptions—two chapters ago, we suggested asking clarifying questions in order to eliminate erroneous assumptions. This bears repeating, however, because while it is easy to read about and understand in a cognitive sense, it is so difficult to accomplish in the heat of the moment. I know this from bitter experience. It is so easy for me to <u>know</u> for a fact what the other person is thinking that I forget to actually find out if my assumption is true. But because perception is reality, my assumption formulates my reaction, and I want to retaliate in such a way that I can guarantee the conflict will escalate, and produce less than positive results. A simple clarifying question might prohibit the discussion from going south, and might actually enhance the relationship instead of wounding it.

Expectations—this is the next logical step after assumptions. Because I approach life and relationships from my own perspective, I have certain expectations of my intimate relational partner. I expect him or her to be like me, think like me, understand where I am coming from, and handle ideas and situations in the same manner in which I do. I expect him or her to be in the same mood I am, to share exactly the same values, and to be on the same wavelength. Above all, I expect him or her not to have expectations of me that I am not aware of (even though it is okay for me to have such expectations). I realize this is beginning to sound confusing and hopelessly philosophical, but please do not lose the point. My expectations of my intimate relational partner can easily produce conflict of a potentially negative nature.

Anxiety—this is a scary emotion. In my entire life, I have never seen a show of hands where people volunteered to be anxiety-ridden for any length of time. A number of years ago, an author by the name of David Augsburger wrote a masterful book entitled, _Caring Enough To Confront_. Let me quote a couple of sentences from that book, because he states it far better than I ever could. "Anger is a demand 'that you recognize my worth.' Actually I first feel anxious. When my freedom to be me is threatened, I become anxious, tense, ready for some action. Anger is much more pleasant to experience than anxiety" (pages 47-48). Confrontation often includes an explosion of anger or even rage. But as you contemplate your anger, think about what might have caused it. Was it an anxious or uneasy feeling that you were not being valued, listened to, or regarded? The intense desire to be rid of anxiety can often cause us to escalate a confrontation experience, even at the expense of a relationship.

I mentioned earlier that one of the erroneous assumptions of conflict is that it must be negative, or win-lose. In closing this section, let me offer an alternative. Patton, Giffin, and Patton, in their book, _Decision Making Group Interaction_, describe two types of conflict—distributive and integrative. Distributive conflict is that which truly exemplifies win-lose results. In other words, someone wins at someone else's expense. This is typically true in sporting events, spelling bees, acting auditions, job interviews, school grades (when the instructor grades on the curve), the lottery, and unfortunately, in many relational situations. While we often attempt to downplay the win-lose aspect of conflict, we are still painfully aware that it exists. There is one winner, and everyone else is a loser. Typically, there is anger, an argumentative spirit, frustration, and bad feelings left over.

On the other hand, with integrative conflict, individuals challenge each other confrontationally, but maintain a mutual and super-ordinate goal whereby both parties "win" and benefit. In other words, the "conflictors" attempt to combine their diverse skills in order that they might both grow and enhance the relationship, which defines winning. They have no desire to achieve 75% success at the other person's 25%, but rather they seek to grow and achieve together, with both realizing maximal development. Please understand that this is not a case of two intimate relational partners attempting to hide or mask their differences or agreeing not to disagree, but honestly challenging and confronting each other in a loving effort to achieve mutual growth. A quick example might solidify the picture.

A corporate marketing team meets to decide on a new advertising campaign, designed to raise their company above the competition. Various members of the team have diverse, and possibly conflicting ideas as to what will be most successful, and each secretly hopes that his or her contributions will be the ones selected. At the same time, they all realize that the ultimate goal is for the corporation to be successful, and so they utilize the conflict in an integrative fashion, allowing for numerous suggestions and brainstorming, hoping to achieve the team goal.

The same is true with integrative conflict with intimate relational partners. The opponent is a strained or broken relationship, or a less than win-win scenario, and the partners lovingly confront each other with fresh and challenging ideas to problem-solve and grow the relationship. This is conflict resolution that is optimal at every level.

Imperative 3
Intentional Listening

I mentioned earlier in this book that the word listen comes from two Anglo-Saxon words which mean "hearing" and "to wait in suspense." In other words, true listening is the kind of thing you do at the end of a movie where the killer's identity is about to be exposed. You wouldn't miss it for the world. I would like to see a show of hands of all those who listen that intently after asking your intimate relationship partner, "How was your day?"

> **"The golden rule of friendship is to listen to others as you would have them listen to you."**
> – *David Augsburger*
> *(quoted in Quotable Quotes, p. 38)*

Research suggests that about 75% of all oral communication is ignored, misunderstood, or quickly forgotten. If I were to tell you that verbally, I would have to say it four times to be sure it was heard and remembered. Hopefully, communication between intimate people alters that percentage significantly, but nevertheless, we have strong evidence to demonstrate that intentional listening is a problem for most of us. Even our formal educational system places reduced emphasis on developing true listening skills. Although I attended school just this side of the Middle Ages, I'm sure many of you can identify with this scenario. I took plenty of classes in writing, many more in reading, and several in speaking. Never once did I take a class in listening, nor do I recall anyone spending much time talking about it (although I may not have been listening at the time).

Since you are reading this book, and not listening to it on tape or being read to you, this may be tricky, but I want to attempt to illustrate a point through the use of two exercises. Look at the triangle below for four or five seconds, then look away and say out loud the words you saw within the triangle.

If you said the words, "Once upon a time," you are incorrect. Look at it again for several more seconds, and then repeat the words you saw. If you still said, "Once upon a time," try the exercise one last time, and then ask your four-year old niece to tell you what the words really are (if it makes you feel better, I think I tried about five times before I realized that it said, "Once upon a a time," with the letter "a" being repeated). Why would intelligent human beings not be able to recognize the four most storied words in children's books? I would suggest it is because we see what we expect to see (perception is reality). The same thing tends to happen when we listen to others—we hear what we expect to hear. Hold that thought for a moment, and read the following paragraph, counting the Fs (both capitals and lower-case) as you go along.

Fred Floffle, a friendly fellow from Florida, founded a flourishing florist shop. He found it fun to frolic with friends while also benefiting from their patronage, which gave him fine profits. Since he had a phenomenal sense of creativity, Fred would often baffle his friends by flowering them with fantastic ferns and other floral arrangements. He was a fantastic man. Unfortunately, the day came when Fred fell sick and died. His faithful friends, full of fabulous admiration for him, formulated an unforgettably beautiful funeral for him, and laid him to rest for the final time in a floral coffin fit for a fully deserving fellow.

How many Fs did you count? 50? 51? 52? 53? Actually, there are 54 Fs in that paragraph. Many people count 52, and realize later that they neglected to count the Fs in the two "of" words. They sounded-out the Fs as they read along, but because the F in the word "of" sounds like a V, they did not count it. The letter F was there, but they missed it because it didn't fit in with the system they had developed.

The analogy here to listening is rather obvious. We don't always hear what someone is saying because we have a different agenda. Since we are focusing on intimate relationship partners only, and not on the general public, or our bosses or politicians, and since this issue, like truth telling and conflict resolution, is the subject for a book all by itself, let me center on only a few key reasons why we don't listen to our significant others as we should. I will call this the FED-UP syndrome.

Familiarity. We think we know the other person so well that we can accurately predict what he or she is going to say, and therefore, we do not listen carefully. This is typically an unconscious act, so it is difficult to combat. Recognition of the tendency is a good place to start, helping us to focus on exactly what the partner is really saying.

Emotions. When we get emotionally wrapped up in the discussion, intentional listening tends to go out the window. We revert to our temperament tendencies, and we attempt to protect our "turf" or egos. This is a good time to press the pause button to be sure we are truly listening, and not reacting because of our feelings.

Detour. Have you ever been listening to an intimate partner, only to have him or her use a word or expression that caused you to take a mental detour and miss the rest of the sentence or entire message? A co-worker mentions a problem she is having with her son, and you think, "Son? Oh, that's right, I have to pick up my son in 20 minutes. Now, how am I going to do that?" The initial detour thoughts are inevitable, but how you choose to dwell on them instead of listening is the key.

Umbrella. I admit this one is a stretch, but I had to come up with a U word. What I mean by umbrella is that we are such busy people that instead of listening intently, we often find ourselves thinking of the myriad of tasks we need to accomplish, or the details we have hanging over our heads and we need to remember. This can be a serious listening burglar, and must be countered by conscious effort.

Preparation. This is the act of being so busy preparing my response to what my partner is saying that I completely miss what he or she has told me. While I am actively involved in the dialogue, in reality it is a monologue because I want to talk and I want him or her to listen. A good way to combat this tendency is to verbally or mentally restate what the other person has said before launching my own response.

If you want to review some ideas on how to become a better listener, turn back to chapter 6 and tour through the STOP sign again. One of the sections is titled, "Listen Actively," but several of the others should also be helpful. In addition, there are any number of communication books available that deal extensively with intentional listening.

Before leaving this topic, let me share one more idea which I have found to be extremely helpful in my quest to be a good listener. I call it listening with my eyes, something which will totally baffle you sense purists. While the example I am about to give does not deal with an intimate relationship partner, it certainly has implications which can be used to more accurately and attentively listen to your significant relations. The kinds of things you will "listen" for with your eyes will be different, but important as you further attempt to focus on what that special person is saying to you.

A number of years ago, I was invited to meet with a Vice President of a rather large corporation in Chicago, to discuss some ideas on continuing education for his employees. As I entered his office, I was determined to listen with my eyes as well as with my ears during our dialogue. The first thing I noticed was that his desk was disgustingly clean, but more important, I observed in one corner of the office an easel with newsprint and five or six markers. My immediate assumption was that he was a teacher at heart, loved to explain and draw diagrams, and liked to have people listen to him. Sure enough, during the course of our conversation, he shared that he was a former school teacher.

Later, while he was explaining his system for orienting new employees, he approached the easel and, utilizing several different colors of the markers, drew his four-part training scheme, which I immediately memorized. We went to lunch about an hour later, and during our meal, he explained to me a program he was designing. I said something like, "That is consistent with your orientation plan," and I repeated the four parts of his diagram. He stared at me for a moment, and I became concerned that I had offended his mother, or had spinach dangling from my teeth. Then he quietly asserted, "You are a very good listener." Well, I'm not always, but that day I was, and it paid big-time dividends. Intentional listening tells people you care about what they say, and with intimate relationship partners, that is a communication imperative.

> ### "Listening, not imitation, may be the sincerest form of flattery."
> ### – Joyce Brothers
> (quoted in <u>Quotable Quotes</u>, p. 124)

Speaking the truth in love, productively resolving the inevitability of conflict, and listening intentionally may not guarantee 100% success in a meaningful relationship, but I know of no better way to start. As we attempt to make US out of ME and YOU, we commit to incorporating the imperatives of communication in our relationship.

CHAPTER 9

♦♦♦

AND THEY LIVED HAPPILY EVER AFTER

"Time will tell"

The past two chapters have dealt with the quest to make US out of ME and YOU. Specifically, we talked about relationship building and communication. We emphasized being feeling, fueling, feeding, and forthright, and we spoke of the communication imperatives of truth telling, conflict resolution, and intentional listening. Before leaving Part 3 of the book, I would like to briefly discuss the critical concept of commitment, to connect with some ideas mentioned in previous chapters.

At some point during the 80s, there was a hit song titled, "When A Man Loves A Woman," which chronicled the lengths to which the author was willing to go in order to prove his love for his lady. Some of the bizarre behavior acts included: not thinking of anything else, spending his very last dime on her, thinking she can do no wrong, trading the world for the good thing he found, turning his back on his best friend if he put her down, and sleeping out in the rain if she wanted him to. Personally, I would have to draw the line at sleeping in the rain, but perhaps that explains why I am currently single. At any rate, the lyrics to the song evidenced the commitment which the author had developed for his intimate relationship partner.

The dictionary defines commitment as a promise or pledge to do something. Most of us have been taught to hold the view that the definition of the word commitment also includes "forever." In other words, to commit to something or someone means to eternally carry out a promise or pledge to do or be something. In real life, that doesn't always work, and some people love to use it as a sledgehammer on others to promote feelings of guilt or inadequacy. Before moving on to more general themes, let me comment on commitment as it relates to marriage and divorce.

Most of us were raised to believe that marriage is a life-time commitment "till death do us part." I whole-heartedly agree with that, as I personally believe that God Himself instituted the marriage relationship, and intended for it to be permanent. Please do not think that I am advocating divorce or other broken relationships. I am not. I have been through a divorce, and it is a very painful experience. I suffered, my former wife suffered, and my boys suffered, and I am aware that the pain will never fully disappear. The last thing I am suggesting is an easy-out from a marriage. But I am also realistic enough to know that people and events change. I made many decisions in my 20s that I moved away from in my 30s and 40s, and some decisions I made in my 30s I am moving away from in my early 50s. The point I am trying to make is this—if you made some "commitments" at some point in your life that you are no longer committed to for any number of reasons, please do not subject yourself to the guilt guillotine. There may be some issues which need to be cleared up, and there may be some areas of your life which need repair, but I would encourage you to refrain from continuously beating yourself up because of your failure to keep a commitment you made.

I am not talking here about someone who consistently makes commitments to others, and then cavalierly disregards them. I am speaking of mature and sincere people who are unable to recover emotionally from a broken commitment at one point in their lives. They allow their own guilt feelings, as well as the continuous reminders from others, to torment them and prevent them from feeling clean, forgiven, and whole. If this characterizes you, and you need professional assistance to deal with it, please get it as soon as possible. Why would you want to be miserable in the future for something you did in the past?

Roger was a man who became a school teacher. He committed his adult life to serving children in that capacity because he had been positively influenced by his elementary school teachers. He was dedicated and effective. Over the course of many years, through unpredictable and negative events, he lost his zeal and burned out. Realizing that his heart was no longer in his classroom, and that he was becoming an unwitting hypocrite, Roger left the teaching profession and became a real estate agent. He never wavered from his belief in education nor turned his back on his desire to give back to others what had been instilled in him. He simply changed careers. The problem was that he beat himself up every day for abandoning his "commitment." He felt he had gone back on his promise to himself to be a life-time educator, and he tortured himself with his own created guilt guillotine.

We hear a lot these days about commitment at work, and how things are not as they once were. Polls indicate that employees today are not as dedicated to the company as were employees in past decades. I attended a business luncheon recently where a woman in the audience asked the speaker (a CEO of an international corporation) a question that went something like this: "Do you think one of the limiting factors regarding employee commitment is the increase of multi-million dollar salary and compensation packages offered to CEOs and Presidents?" The speaker admitted that the disparity in compensation between management and labor impacted the level of dedication workers felt toward their jobs.

According to the AFL-CIO's Executive Pay Watch Web site, between 1980 and 1995, CEO pay rose 500%. By 1997, CEOs in the United States made an average of 209 times the pay of the average factory worker. In the same vein, I read a story in one of the Chicago newspapers about a lady who worked for a company which enjoyed lofty morale on the part of its employees. In fact, the article stated that people were like a family, and went out of their way to help each other. Then the company was sold, and people were downsized, and benefits were slashed. The mood among employees bordered on disbelief and depression. The lady arrived at an interesting conclusion—the importance of creating a distinction between attachment and commitment. She posited, "You need to be committed to your work, but not attached to your job or even the company you work for. Nothing is guaranteed and you have to be able to let go when you have to."

"It's strange how unimportant your job is when you're asking for a raise, but how important it can be when you want to take a day off."
– Earl A. Mathes
(quoted in Quotable Quotes, p. 117)

Let me share something with you to see if it can be as helpful to you as it is to me. I am committed to many specifics in my life, among which are my sons, education, saving money, and teaching eager students. I am also committed to some more general ideas—being happy, life-long learning, my faith, and helping others. But there are three concepts to which I am deeply committed, and they are the very backbone of this book. These are truth, respect, and relationships.

Concept 1
Truth

I am committed to being truthful with my intimate relationship partners, whether they be family members or friends. I will not elaborate on this, as we discussed it more thoroughly in the last chapter. But this is a commitment I have made—to be intentionally honest, and to speak the truth in love. I would encourage you to make the same commitment, if you have not already done so. In my opinion, without truth telling at all times, relationships are a facade and a farce. To be involved in a "non-truthful intimate relationship" is an oxymoron. If it is not truthful, it is not an intimate relationship, although we pretend it is. Commit to truth-telling, and also to truth-hearing. If you choose not to hear the truth from your partner, I have the same question about the relationship. Some things are baseline and cannot be missing or disposed of.

Concept 2
Respect

I am committed to respect, not just with my intimate relationship partners, but with all people. This is certainly easier to do with partners, but on various levels, I am committed to respect everyone, even the THEMs in my life, and we will discuss that in the last section of this book. I may not always agree with my intimate relationships (in fact, I'd <u>better</u> not always agree, or none of us will grow), but I will respect them and honor them and hold them in highest esteem. Some of my intimate relationship partners are smarter than others, some are more loving than others, some are more creative than others, some are more athletic than others, and some are more perceptive than others. I respect each of them for their unique gifts and talents and abilities and temperaments, but I absolutely respect all of them equally for their very selves. My life would be incomplete if any one of them were to vanish.

I would encourage you to commit yourself to respect, if you have not already done so. And here is the kicker, and it just might make you feel very uncomfortable, but remember, I am committed to truth-telling. If you identify one of your intimate relationship partners and say, "I truthfully cannot respect him or her," then please do an assessment of your relationship. Is it truly a relationship, or does it just look like one? Do you actually relate, or just talk? Do you really "live" with this person, or merely co-exist? These are difficult questions, but a truth-telling, truth-seeking, honest, relationship-oriented, respectful person will ask them, and will seek appropriate answers.

"I get no respect from my dog. The other day, the dog went to the door and started to bark. I went over and opened it. The dog didn't want to go out; he wanted me to leave."
– Rodney Dangerfield
(quoted in Quote Unquote, p. 276)

The idea of respect deals not only with the respect we have for others, but also, and actually first and foremost, the respect we have for ourselves. Think back to Chapter 1 when we asserted that if I do not truly understand myself, I will have no clue how to understand others, even my most intimate relationship partners. This is why Part 1 of this book had to precede Part 2 of this book. If I do not know myself, I cannot know you. If I do not love myself, I cannot love you. And if I do not respect myself, I cannot respect you.

This is so simple that many of us miss it. We are so busy trying to fix other people that we do not recognize how badly we need fixing. When my former wife and I were first experiencing some problems with our marriage, we had dinner with a husband and wife team of counselors, who were also our friends. After much questioning and probing, the counseling wife said to me, "I don't think you love your wife. I don't think you love your parents. I don't think you love yourself. In fact, I don't think you are currently capable of loving anyone." This, of course, was less than encouraging to hear, but she was probably right. I did not love myself, so how was I going to know how to love other people?

It took me many years to begin to love myself, and I'm not sure I have it entirely right yet. I still struggle with it, probably just like you do. As I stated in the Preface, this is why I have written this book. I would love to state that I have my act together, but I still flounder in the pool of the struggling, attempting to stay afloat. I have discovered during my many years of teaching adult students that they learn better from each other than they do from me. So please accept my ideas and suggestions as those offered by a fellow journeyman, not an expert who has arrived.

Most of us are familiar with Abraham Maslow (Psychology 101) and his hierarchy of needs as motivators in our lives. I will not bore you with a recount of the various stages, but Maslow states that until we have passed through the stage of needing love and belonging from others, we cannot attain the stage of respect, both from self and others. What he is saying is that if I need others to like or affirm me, then I have not reached the stage of seeking respect from them or from myself. As the story goes, a man approached a woman in a night club and asked her to dance. She replied, "No way, Bozo. Get out of my face." He retorted, "Then I suppose a formal date is out of the question, right?" People join groups or clubs or gangs in order to belong, to feel liked and accepted. It is only after that need has been fulfilled that they focus on being respected. Let me illustrate with a personal example.

When I first began teaching adult students in 1979, I wanted very much to have them like me. I was barely older than most of them, and younger than some, and it was of extreme importance to me that they accept me and shower me with excellent evaluations. I remember compromising with some of my academic standards so that they would not be angry with me. I needed to be needed. I liked to be liked. After a few years, I became less concerned with how much I was liked, and began to concentrate more on how well I was respected as an intelligent professional. I no longer pussyfooted with requirements or grades, but became more demanding of the students because I was more concerned with being respected than liked.

In more recent years, I have been more cognizant of my need to respect myself, even if the students do not respect me (although not surprisingly, self-respect and respect from others typically go hand in hand). I have concentrated more on their learning and growth, and not on how they view me. I have learned to speak the truth in love, conveying to the student that, "You are a wonderful human being, and I like you immensely, but your work is not college level. I will help you, but you must make the effort to achieve an acceptable performance." This is the essence of self-respect, moving past the need to be liked, to look in the mirror and admire what you see.

Concept 3
Relationships

I am committed to relationships. Please note how I worded that. While individual and specific relationships may come and go over time (relocation, divorce, irreconcilable differences or arguments, death), I am committed to the concept of relationships. I believe that it is not good for people to be alone. We are socially-oriented, and we crave interaction from others. As noted in Chapters 1 and 2, there are differences between introverts and extraverts, but we all share the common desire to be in relationship with others. Sometimes I like to be alone, but I never like to be lonely. This is the chief reason why shopping malls are so incredibly popular. People will meander from store to store for hours, never looking for anything in particular, and never making a purchase, all because they want to be around other people. Many years ago, I had breakfast with a college President who was on the road most of the time, fund-raising for his school. He tried to explain to me how lonely it got in hotel rooms. He told me that at times, he would go to the hotel lobby and sit in a chair for an hour or so, just to be around other people.

Do you think computers, on-line everything, and the internet will revolutionize our society in terms of replacing social interaction? I don't. I have had dozens of students tell me that they would never take a college degree program that was totally on-line because they crave the interaction of their classmates. Group interaction over the computer and chat-rooms will have their place, but they will never displace the face-to-face encounters we have grown to love.

Crutch, Convenience, Companion

Let's talk about commitment in relationships, but first I would once again encourage you to examine the most intimate relationships you have, to be certain that they are true relationships and not appearance-only clusters. If they are less than relational, some serious thinking is in order. I have discovered in my life that if I am in a "relationship" that is not truly relational, then the other person (partner?) is a crutch, a convenience, or a companion. Take these in reverse order.

A companion is someone you walk down the road with until it is time for one of you to exit the highway for your destination. A companion is fleeting, there is mutual benefit, but don't count on the long-range relationship.

A convenience is not necessarily mutually beneficial. It is someone who provides you with what you need at the moment (friendship, money, children, status, sex), but everything is a one-way street, unless both parties are using the other as a convenience. "Using" is the key word here, and convenience relationships are pathetic and sick. Unfortunately, they are also prevalent and often subconscious. Do you remember my earlier comment about women students of mine whose husbands begrudge them returning to school because of their own twisted egos, and needs to be superior? That is a convenient "relationship." Keep her home. Keep her down. Keep her pregnant. Keep her dependent. Keep me looking good because I have a respectable marriage to go along with my career. When I need her to be with me in public, she'll be there. When I want her opinion, I'll rattle her cage. When I need assistance with the little and unimportant decisions for which I have no time, I'll delegate them to her. She is so convenient. Gosh, what a great relationship we have!

A crutch is someone you need because you can't make it alone. A crutch may be smoothing, docile, enabling, co-dependent, or a seeing-eye dog. A crutch is similar to a convenience, except that it contains the concept of necessity. If Joann and Carl have a convenience relationship, then either one of them can terminate it when it is no longer convenient. But if Carl is a crutch for Joann, she cannot end the relationship because she needs him, or she needs to replace him with a substitute crutch. As with a companion or a convenience, a crutch may appear to others to be an equal partner in a healthy relationship, but in fact is not. The association is not relational.

We Are All Committed To Something

Believe it or not, we are all committed to something. The professional athlete who turns down more money from another team in order to remain with the team that has been fair to him is committed to loyalty. The professional athlete who abandons his team in order to sign on with a team that will pay him more money is committed to something else, like financial security for his family or better opportunities for himself. The professional athlete who turns down $50 million offered by his team because another team will pay him $52 million is committed to, well, you tell me. The school teacher who remains in a low-paying position in a crime-infested school is typically committed to her students or educational principles in general.

> *"I have a dream."*
> *– Dr. Martin Luther King Jr.*

When I was in high school and college in the 60s, it was the "in" thing to be committed to a cause, whether it be free speech, civil rights, or political freedom. For many of us, however, commitment was not fully understood. As long as there were rallies and marches, commitment was a pretty cool thing, but if it involved going to jail, that was another story entirely. I think it was at that time that I learned to greatly admire and respect Dr. Martin Luther King, and I learned vicariously what it meant to be truly committed to a cause. To be repeatedly arrested and jailed, to be subjected to vicious taunts and threats, to have my house burned to the ground—that was not my idea of a good time. And the possibility of assassination sent many lesser people toward a quieter cause.

There is an old joke about a conversation between a chicken and a pig. They were discussing that breakfast favorite, ham and eggs. The pig declared, "For you, eggs are a contribution. For me, ham is a commitment."

As I share a few thoughts about commitment within a relationship, let me repeat what I have mentioned several times previously. This one is real important, and we need to get it right. We need to honestly ask ourselves if the relationship is important enough to be absolutely committed to. If it is not, then the rest of this is rather meaningless, and one of three things should happen: the relationship should end, we should continue to live out the lie and facade (of companion, convenience or crutch partners), or we should return to square one and attempt to rebuild the relationship to the point where commitment is desirable.

Countdown to Commitment

As I close this section on commitment, please remember that I am speaking of all types of relationships, not just marriage. The important elements of commitment are applicable to relationships between spouses, family members, other loved ones, friends, and significant others in our lives who help make US out of ME and YOU. In that regard, think about several of the US relationships you have. As we go through the countdown to commitment, discuss these with your intimate relationship partners to see if they might be helpful. Actually, nothing here is new. We have discussed all of these ideas in previous sections of this book. However, I have listed them here as a group because I feel quite strongly that they are the crux to cementing a commitment to any worthy relationship. Here is the countdown to blasting off into the world of relational commitment.

5) Always assume good intentions on the part of your intimate relationship partner. Suspicion and mistrust do not go well with commitment. If this proves to be difficult, I would once again hit the pause button to reflect on the nature of the relationship. Since we are talking only about our special YOUs, I am making the assumption that there is a tried-and-true trust factor already in place. In my experience, I have found that assuming good intentions works two ways. Not only does it constantly reinforce my own commitment, but it is catching. The more I assume that my partner has only honorable and best intentions, the more he or she believes the same about me. Eventually, this becomes an unconscious thing, and it is unthinkable that he or she would do anything other than have the best of intentions.

4) In any disagreement or confrontation, always separate the person from the issue or cause of the conflict. This logically follows on the heels of #5 (and leads directly into #3), but it is sometimes more difficult to remember during the heat of the moment. Can you seriously disagree with someone, while simultaneously loving the person unconditionally, and totally refraining from personal attack?

Of course, you assert that you can and do. Let me provide you with a dilemma. You have a spouse or very close friend. Each of you works for different companies, both of which are about to experience a strike which has been bitter, and will cost a great deal of money. One of you is labor, and the other is management. Will you be able to discuss the situations without either or both of you resorting to less-than-commitment type communication? If so, you are to be congratulated on your commitment to your relationship.

3) Never intentionally say or do anything which will cause physical or psychological harm to your intimate relationship partner. Please understand that I used the word "intentionally." All of us, from time to time, accidentally say hurtful things, or make mistakes which result in other people being inconvenienced, pressured, or harmed. It is at this point that your partner needs to practice #5 above, and assume your best intentions. Unfortunately, some of us become frustrated, even with our most significant others, and cannot resist the urge to "zing" him or her with a well-placed barb or criticism. We succumb to the temptation because, at the moment, we feel violated or anxiety-ridden, and while we may later rue the comment, the damage has already been done. What follows next is painfully obvious—the more we resort to intentional abuse, the more difficult it becomes for our partner to always assume our good intentions. And the cycle begins all over again.

2) Agree with your partner to use the STOP sign from chapter 6 in your interactions with each other. At that point, we spoke of it as an effective tool to use in combating the habit of assuming benign ignorance on the part of others. However, in a more sophisticated way, the STOP sign can work wonders in assisting intimate relationship partners to demonstrate commitment to each other. All eight of the points on the sign are applicable here. Read them aloud several times with your partner. Discuss their merits. Add to them if that might be helpful to you. Eliminate the ones you believe are not appropriate to your situation. Above all, regularly practice the ones which you need in your relationship. Allow for failures and mistakes. Celebrate when you successfully demonstrate your learnings. Use as many interaction and communication aids as possible to further deepen your commitment to your important relationships.

1) Turn failures into victories. Convert distributive conflict into integrative conflict. Accept the difficulties of effective communication, and allow them to be teaching tools. Struggle together. Learn together. Share the defeats, and mutually find a way to turn them into opportunities for growth. When a good orchestra or choir suffers from a poor performance, the members do not sit around the practice room, pointing fingers at each other and renouncing their commitment to the ensemble. They regroup, review what went wrong, re-commit to each other, and plan how they will improve the performance next time. This is what separates good teams from weak teams, and the same is true in good relationships and weak ones. Losers mope while winners cope. And by the way, there is more good news. When relationship partners commit to growing from difficulties, the relationship becomes stronger and stronger with each passing test, and the commitment concrete becomes harder and harder until it is impenetrable. Do you remember a song by Neil Sedaka titled, "Breaking Up Is Hard To Do?" One of the lines was, "Instead of breaking up, I wish that we were making up again." That is what commitment is, and in some relationships, making up can be lots of fun!

Blastoff!

Temperament and Commitment

Thinkers and feelers often regard commitment differently, and word it according to their types. Thinkers have a tendency to hold tenaciously to a commitment because it is the right thing to do, while feelers tend to be committed because of personal involvement and emotions. Both are legitimate, and both types will feel guilty if they back out of a commitment, but they will experience guilt for different reasons. Feelers will focus on how the other person reacts or is affected (how would I feel if someone did that to me?), and thinkers will focus on the bottom line (what will be the result of this broken commitment?) or the logical conclusion that backing out of a commitment will cause pain, discomfort, or inconvenience which must be redressed. Let me illustrate.

Early in my marriage, my wife and I agreed to assist her former roommate and husband move from one apartment to another. They had also asked three other couples to help, and it was to be a kind of party. When we showed up, we were the only ones who followed through on the promise to help. The others all had excuses why they couldn't be there. As a thinker, I remember saying to myself, "It would never dawn on me to back out of this promise. What if everyone did (and they did)? How would the job get done?" Never once did it cross my mind how our friends might be feeling about people bailing out on them in a time of need. I was there because it was right to be there, and I was focused on the job at hand.

The reason I am mentioning this thinker-feeler difference is because of the way intimate relationship partners might react to hearing how the other person describes commitment or is bound by it (and please pay attention to this because it is very important). Feelers might question, "You mean your commitment to me is based on logic, right and wrong, cold principles, and not on how you feel about me as a friend, family member, spouse, or lover? What happens if your logic changes? Where does that leave me?" Thinkers might question, "You mean your commitment to me is based on how you feel about me, without regard to the rightness of dedication, or a principle-centered view of commitment? What happens if your feelings change? Where does that leave me?"

If you need to review chapter 2 for an understanding of how thinkers and feelers approach issues, please do so. A misunderstanding of how people view commitment can cause unnecessary divisions within a relationship. As the intimate relationship partners discuss the concept in depth, they should understand that they are both saying the same thing, using different words and approaches. Focus on the commonalities, and the differences will dissipate like a vapor.

Commitment Focus

Relationships that feature commitment are different from other kinds of relationships in that their focus is timeless. By that I mean they focus on the past, the present, and especially the future. They celebrate the past by laughing uproariously over humorous events and embarrassing moments. They live the present by insisting that every day is a good day for the relationship. They eagerly anticipate the future by dreaming growth dreams and planning growth plans. There is a vitality in a relationship which features commitment that is noticeably vacant in other relationships. It is hard to describe, but it is unmistakable. It is not stagnant, but exudes vibrancy, excitement, and possibilities. It is a commitment not just to the union (which may be cold and distant and formal), but to the relationship (which is alive and active and growing). The wife of a famous American was once asked if she ever entertained thoughts of divorcing him. She quipped, "No. I thought about murdering him, but never divorcing him." It was meant to be light-hearted, but how many "relationships" tend to be like that?

I want to make one more commitment comment about my own relationship with my former wife. When we separated and divorced, we committed to each other that we would never air our differences in front of our boys, that we would never demean each other, put each other down, use each other to further our own ends, or attempt in any way to drive a wedge which might require our boys to take sides, or psychologically choose one parent over the other. While our commitment to each other ended, our commitment to our sons is eternal, and we both strive with all we have to cement those precious relationships.

Interestingly, a couple of years ago, one of the boys' friends, whose parents are also divorced, made a comment to them that went something like this: "You guys are so lucky that your parents get along. Your dad comes over to the house and talks to your mom, and they discuss plans for you, and agree on what is going to be done. If my mom and dad ever got in the same house, one of them would not come out alive." That is so tragic. Why should innocent people have to suffer because of broken relationships? Some commitments entered into voluntarily are not life-long, even if they were meant to be. This is true of marriage, business, or friendships. But commitments to innocent people, especially children, are a different breed entirely. These commitments are inviolate.

Confirm Commitment

Let me close this chapter by making a suggestion. Identify the intimate relationship partners in your life, and ask them the following questions:

- "What about my behavior confirms to you that I am committed to our relationship?"

- "Is there anything about my behavior that causes you to question my commitment to our relationship?"

I am not suggesting asking these questions in order to open up an opportunity for argument or strain within the relationship. I am offering this idea as a way of confirmation. Most people I know (myself included) suffer from insecurity. From time to time, we have a tendency to question whether or not our relationships are as solid and permanent as we think. So I am suggesting discussing these questions.

Hopefully, the purpose in asking those questions would be to seek honest feedback and to keep the train on the track, not to elicit suspicion ("What have you done?"), or initiate an argument ("Of course I am committed to you. I pay the bills, mow the lawn, take out the garbage, help you with your homework, cover for you at work, buy you presents for your birthday, baby sit for your kids, coach your team, cook your meals. What is the point of this question?")

In a healthy relationship, confirmation of commitment is not negative in nature, nor an attempt to continuously reinforce hopeless insecurities. It is rather a celebration of the relationship, an outgrowth of pure joy and exuberance, and we can live happily ever after.

SUMMARY OF PART 3

In this section of the book, we have attempted to combine ME and YOU into US. We have concentrated on the most important and meaningful relationships in our lives. We have focused on what makes our most significant relationships so special, and we have investigated what actions are necessary to witness their survival and growth. We have seen how to be feeling, fueling, feeding, and forthright, and we have realized that in each case, commitment to the relationship is the key element.

We have glanced at three crucial elements in any meaningful relationship—truth telling, conflict resolution, and intentional listening. We have emphasized the power of the words, "Speak the truth in love." We have understood that conflict is not always a negative thing, but can be utilized by intimate relational partners to clarify issues, correct misunderstandings, and promote growth within the relationship. We have explored the difficult task of truly listening to each other in an attempt to solidify our most meaningful interactions.

We have boldly approached the delicate concept of commitment. We have recognized that in any lasting interactions, we must be committed to truth, respect, and relationships. Most of us can identify people we know (hopefully not ourselves) who are embedded in "relationships" that are really crutches, conveniences, or companions. We have examined five important steps on the countdown to commitment, and we have discussed ways to confirm our own commitment to the intimate relationship partners in our lives.

We now come to the last section of the book, which will focus on the THEMs in our lives, all the other people who are not YOUs to us. It would be easy to gloss over these individuals, since they are not within our inner circles, but I think that would be a mistake. In fact, I believe the ultimate test of relationship building is with those we typically ignore, evaluate, or discount, due to our lack of knowledge or understanding of them. But in order to come full-circle in the world of relationships, we would serve ourselves well to spend quality time considering THEMs. That is where we will now turn our attention.

PART 4

CHAPTER 10

◆◆◆

THEY SEEM TO BE EVERYWHERE

"Ubiquity is all over the place"

In the final section of this book, we are going to focus on the THEMs in our lives. With sincere apologies to all of the English teachers who worked so diligently to educate me over many years, THEMs are people who are not YOUs to us. THEMs are people who we work with (but share no intimate relationship), ride the bus with, pass in the grocery store, wait behind for hours at the local fast food restaurant, sit next to at the ball game, watch on television or at the movies, vote for (or against), read about in the newspaper, take our toll money, teach our kids, fix our appliances, sell us shoes, give us speeding tickets, deliver our pizza, and make laws by which we have to live. Some THEMs we know, some we don't. Some we like and respect, some we don't. Some THEMs we deal with every day, some we see only once in a lifetime, and some we never meet at all.

For the purposes of what I would like to discuss in the remaining chapters of this book, it might be helpful to categorize the THEMs in our lives. I have taken the liberty of classifying THEMs into two camps: the THEMs we know and with whom we interact, and the THEMs we don't know. The first group consists of all the people who have a place in our lives, but with whom we do not maintain an intimate relationship, and therefore are not YOUs to us. These are friends (or possibly relatives who are not close), co-workers, neighbors, people we speak with on a regular basis, or have contact with from time to time.

The second group consists of all the people who do not have a place in our lives. This group could be considered rather vast, as it potentially could include everyone on the planet. It could include someone as close as the driver of the car next to you in the traffic snarl on the expressway, or someone as distant as a field worker in Nigeria. Movie stars would be included in this group (unless you know them personally), as would professional athletes, TV news commentators, politicians, authors, or other public figures. I mention this because even though you recognize their names, and may even know quite a bit about them, they are still distant THEMs because you do not have personal contact with them, and you do not in any way impact their lives, nor they your life.

Hopefully, you have figured out by now that this book is all about relationships, both with self and others. We have discussed, first and foremost, understanding ourselves. We have then talked about attempting to understand the important people in our lives. We then moved into the delicate area of relating to these important and intimate people. Now we want to think about how we can best relate to the rest of humanity, and this last leg of the journey should bring us back full-circle. By that I mean that if I cannot relate appropriately to the THEMs in my life, then I probably need to return to Chapter 1 in order to re-examine who I am, and what I am all about.

Please do not miss or gloss over this crucial point. I may be able to relate quite well to the YOUs in my life, and I may be enormously successful in my relationships with my intimate relationship partners, but if I cannot relate appropriately to my THEMs, I have missed a key component in this whole scenario. I would bet the mortgage that if I fail to maintain successful relationships with people who are not intimately close to me, then I am deficient in understanding who I really am. This may not make perfect sense at this point, but I trust that within the next three chapters, it will be abundantly clear what I am emphasizing. To have a mature and accurate picture of who I really am, and to accept myself for who I am, is to be able to understand and relate to those who I do not know.

I am not much of a card player, and I have dabbled in Blackjack on only a few occasions (and then only for fun, not for real money, as I am not a gambler or risktaker). But from my infrequent soirees at the table, I remember terms like "hit me" and "stay." Hit me is aggressive action, moving forward confidently. Stay is passive inaction, remaining conservatively in place. One is "go" while the other is "stop." Similarly, when I manage my sons' high school park district baseball team, we have signs to instruct the players on what to do while at bat or running the bases. We have a "swing away" sign and a "take" sign. We have a "steal" sign and a "don't steal" sign. One is go while the other is stop. In this chapter, I would like to focus on the "go" of how to relate to the THEMs in our lives, and in the next chapter, I would like to emphasize how we might best "stop" in order to maintain those relationships.

Hit Me

In the previous section of this book, when we concentrated on the US part of our lives, we focused mainly on three concepts: relationship-building, communication, and commitment. I would like to boldly make the assertion that we owe the same three considerations to the THEMs in our lives, although obviously in different ways. Right now, you are probably entertaining some questions in your mind (and if you are not, you probably should be). These questions might go something like this:

- "Am I supposed to have a relationship with someone I don't know?"
- "How can I communicate with someone in Outer Mongolia when I don't even like Mongolian beef chop suey?"
- "What commitment do I owe to someone with whom I have no interaction or discourse?"
- "I can understand relationship-building, communication, and commitment with a YOU in my life, but how does this flesh out with people I don't really know, or may never see?"

Actually, these are very good questions. Let's take them one at a time.

Relationship-Building

Building relationships with people who are special and intimate makes a lot of sense, but why should I be concerned with having a relationship with someone who I don't even know? That is a poser, for sure. Let me respond in two ways. First, with regard to the THEMs who we do know, at least superficially, attempting to build a relationship could possibly blossom into a YOU relationship, or at least a more positive THEM relationship. As we treat others with respect, inquire about their lives, attempt to understand them as precious human beings, and genuinely appreciate them for their "personhood," we gain knowledge from their experiences, and we learn in ways that we could not learn alone. In addition, occasionally we discover ways in which we might mutually benefit along with each other. Let me provide an illustration of this concept.

As I have mentioned previously, I enjoy managing my sons' baseball team each year. For the past three years, I have seen another manager from time to time. I instantly labeled him as aloof, somewhat conceited, and someone who thought himself to be above me because he had more experience in the league, and knew more people. But all that changed a few weeks ago.

He and I engaged in a telephone conversation about an up-coming game, discovered that we shared some talents and abilities, realized that our life goals were somewhat parallel, and met for breakfast to determine whether we might be able to work together in a mutually beneficial way. He has been a superb gentleman for many years—I just didn't realize it because I never had a relationship with him. Last year he was a distant THEM in my life, but now he is a close THEM to me. While we don't have an intimate relationship, we have mutual respect and understanding, and we desire to get to know each other better, and to work together if it is in both of our best interests.

What if I had clung to my assumptions that he was aloof, conceited, and unapproachable? What if I had discussed only the up-coming ball game, and not spoken with him about our careers and plans? I would have missed out on an opportunity to possibly further my own career interests as well as his, but far more importantly, I would have missed out on an opportunity to know someone better, to appreciate his gifts, to realize that his life struggles are similar to my own, to bond with a fellow-traveler on this road we call life. I am so grateful for that experience in relationship-building.

What occurs with youth baseball experiences can be multiplied many times over in other venues, if we are willing to seek for the opportunities to develop relationships. I have met people on airplanes (distant THEMs) who have become friends or network partners because of a brief, but sincere, conversation. It can happen at schools, in clubs, on subway stations, or at soccer games. I could cite a number of examples where I have worked with people for several years without really knowing who they were, but over a chance lunch, realized what we had in common, and developed a bond.

But what if relationships do not form as quickly or smoothly as mine did with the baseball manager, or what if I have so many things going in my life that I really do not want any further relationships? In that case, what do I owe relationship-wise to the THEMs in my life? I would suggest that what we owe is respect, and to treat the other person as we would want THEMs to treat us. This, of course, is called the Golden Rule, and while it is a no-brainer in a cognitive sense, most of us violate it on a daily basis. I will mention this again in the next chapter, when we discuss the "stop" side of relating to THEMs, but for now, let me elaborate on what I mean by respect and treating the other person as I would want to be treated by him or her.

OK, I respect you—now get out!

Have you ever witnessed how parents interact with an umpire at their children's baseball game? I personally have never heard such abuse heaped upon an individual in any situation which did not feature critical outcomes. The parents (never us managers, by the way) will literally scream, threaten, and spew profanities which they have ordered their kids never to utter, and on occasions you will read in the newspaper how an umpire was physically attacked after a game and beaten by angry parents. Of course this action is staged right in front of their children, who are then directed to participate in the handshake line with the opposite team members. The poor umpire, usually just a kid himself, is making about $15 per game, and is doing the best job he can do. He is intimidated by much older adults (chronologically speaking), and shown no respect. In the heat of the moment, they fail to take into consideration that he is someone else's son, and he is performing his task to the best of his ability.

This scenario was brought home to me most vividly several years ago when my own boys became involved in umpiring games for young players. I attended several of the games to watch the umpire. I sat in the make-shift stands with the parents, who had no clue that the umpire was my son (despite my constant comments like, "Good call, Ump," and my banner which read, "The umpire is your friend.") But every time he made a close call which went against their team, I could hear the snide remarks. "Where did they get this kid, anyway? He doesn't even know the rules. He is missing calls right and left." I so badly wanted to grip their throats and rip out their vocal chords. Didn't they know that he was really a nice kid just trying to do a good job and make a few bucks?

This is what I mean by respect—attempting to look past my tunnel vision of the current scenario and treating the other person as a human being. Let me provide another example. Several weeks ago, one of my students presented to the class her research study of the practice of polygamy in some African countries. It was a fascinating report, and the usual quips were offered—"I can't even afford one wife, let alone several," or "I've also had three wives, just not all at the same time." But what struck me was the energy and effort it takes to truly respect a system that we do not subscribe to and maybe cannot even understand.

For many of us, our instantaneous reaction to something like that is to consider it primitive and beneath our standards. While we may be polite enough to keep those feelings to ourselves, they are still there, and the tendency is to criticize rather than attempt to understand and respect a culture which thrives on systems which we do not practice. Can you imagine the chuckles in other countries when they hear about much of our lifestyle idiosyncrasies? Actually, we are just catching up. Most African tribes were body-piercing centuries ago.

If you find it difficult to make your initial reaction to a THEM a positive or respectful one, allow me to offer a suggestion that has worked for me for several years. Please understand, I have not perfected this art. In fact, I continue to fail more than I succeed, but I am getting better. Refer back several paragraphs to where I was speaking of my son as an umpire. What I attempt to do is to remember that every THEM to me is a YOU to someone else. This may be an unknown person to me, and I want to label, criticize, judge, and maybe even detest, but to someone else this is a treasured human being. To someone else, this may be the most precious person in the galaxy. When I view the individual through those lenses, my tendency is to be more respectful and appreciative, more tolerant and understanding.

> *To everybody, a certain person on earth is the most important person on earth.*

I want to take this one step further. I have this really strange habit, which some of my friends wish to diagnose, but so far there are no medical or psychological terms to identify the disease. Often, when I am in a crowd of people, I will focus on one individual, and wonder about his or her life.

- What are this person's goals, fears, desires, hopes, problems, concerns?
- What have his or her experiences been to this point in life?
- Does this person have friends, or is he or she lonely?
- To whom is this the most important person in the world?

I am the first to admit that this is a somewhat bizarre activity (although it serves the purpose of passing time while waiting for the light to turn green), but what it has done for me is to help me focus on the good and positive side of people. Over time, it has enabled me to begin observing others in a more respectful light. More now than in the past, I tend to react to others with care, respect, and understanding that their life circumstances may not be as fortunate as my own. I want to do unto other THEMs as I would want those THEMs to do unto me.

Communication

Here is another no-brainer for you. If I enter into a respectful relationship with those individuals who I do not know, it will most certainly alter how I communicate with them. Think back to the umpire story of a few paragraphs ago. If you understand that the person is someone else's son, the most important person in someone's life, and a truly nice individual who is trying to do his job to the best of his ability, how likely will you be to stand up and shout, "You're blind, you moron! You have the brains of a fence post?"

The method of communication follows closely the level of relationship. Let me say that again. The method of communication follows closely the level of relationship. If I overhear two colleagues arguing vehemently with each other, not listening to the other, evidencing tunnel vision, and striving to prove a point, it does not take me long to discern their level of relationship with each other. Where there is lack of respect, there will be lecture, criticism, and judgment, but there will not be effective communication. Where there is lack of relationship, there will be attack, inattentiveness, and bullying, but there will not be effective communication.

On the other hand, if I overhear two colleagues confronting each other with attentive ears, clarifying questions, and respectful attitudes, I know instantly that the level of relationship is good, and that the conversation will produce positive results. Relationship always precedes communication, and communication is a true indicator of what the relationship is.

How can you communicate **WELL** when the relationship is **SICK?**

Several chapters ago, we discussed communication between intimate relationship partners. As with relationship-building, I would suggest that we utilize the same principles for effective communication with THEMs, although with different intensity and personal involvement. The three areas we covered were: truth telling, conflict resolution, and intentional listening. As I observe interactions between THEMs (usually in the workplace), I typically witness more failure than success regarding effective communication. I wish this were not the case, but unfortunately, ego often overshadows maturity, and "winning" (distributive conflict) overshadows team victory (integrative conflict).

Many people I know describe the workplace as a zoo. If that is the case, let me introduce you to some of the animals I have observed in the corporate menagerie, along with their communication styles.

Cubicle 1: The Foxes

These are the manipulators. They are sly and clever, and will communicate with you in such a way so as to confuse or baffle you. The Foxes have a definite hidden agenda in most conversations, and their chief aim is to get their own way, even at your expense. They will usually attempt to convince you that they have your best interest at heart, and that they seek win-win solutions to problems, but as you observe them over time, you understand that they have orchestrated a well-thought-out plan for making themselves successful. They put one arm around your shoulder, but only to draw you closer because they tote short knives.

Cubicle 2: The Mice

These are the timid "yes-men," filled with trepidation. They know exactly what to say in order to survive in the dog-eat-dog world. They go-along in order to get-along. They tell you your dress looks good on you when it would look better on fire. They fear for their occupational lives, and shy away from being truthful, lest they pay a penalty for candor or honesty. When I was a kid, there was a cigarette commercial featuring someone with a black eye, and the slogan was, "I'd rather fight than switch." The Mice would rather switch than fight. Weak leaders surround themselves with Mice, but eventually fail because their doomed ideas are not challenged.

Cubicle 3: The Chameleons

These are the people who crawl around, looking for the next rear end to kiss. They are different from the Mice in that they are not so fearful of termination, but rather they wish to elevate themselves via the coat-tail route. They tell you what they know you want to hear so that you will assume loyalty, and take them with you on your rise to stardom. However, they also communicate with your chief rival in the same vein. During the Viet Nam war, there were Chameleons known as Border Bandits, who would sell information to the highest bidder. At work, Chameleons latch onto the person who is one rung higher on the success ladder than the others, but they keep close tabs on position changes. They are fun to watch at basketball games. They root hard for whichever team is leading at the moment, they alter loyalties dozens of times during the game, and their team always wins.

Cubicle 4: The Ostriches

These are the blamers and complainers, the ones who cannot see their own faults or inadequacies because their responsibility heads are buried in the sand. Instead, they focus attention on the shortcomings of others or the system in general. "Of course I failed—how could anyone succeed in a company as screwed-up as this one is?" The Ostriches believe the entire world is out of step with them. They tend to produce little effort, and even less achievement, but it is always someone else's fault. Ostriches will bombard you with "ain't it awful" scenarios. Rather than fix a problem, they scurry around trying to find someone to blame it on. Certainly, they had nothing to do with it. Ostriches can be not only demoralizing, but fatal. If you work with some (and who doesn't?), avoid them like the plague. They will sap your energy, deplete your enthusiasm, and abort your initiative. Don't let them bring you down to their pathetic level.

Cubicle 5: The Bulls

These are the intimidators, which I applaud if they reside in Chicago, are the six-time NBA champions, and my home-town favorites, but at the workplace, the Bulls are an entirely different story. I have long insisted that intimidation is the highest form of cowardice. If you must bully someone into obedience or compliance, then your leadership or managerial efforts are beneath dignity. The intimidators are the ones who assert their power (by position, not by personality) because they are acutely aware that they are not respected or liked by those whom they govern. They tell you what to think, when to think it, and how to think it. They know that without intimidation, they are powerless to lead. In fact, they <u>cannot</u> lead, because leading assumes that there are followers. With intimidating communicators, there are no followers, only Mice or Chameleons, or Foxes, or Ostriches. I once reported to a Bull who felt compelled to correct a subordinate who had made a mistake. He boastfully related to me that his comment to her was, "You get two mistakes with me, and you already have made your first one!" On a scale of one to ten, how loyal do you think she was toward him after their "conversation?" This will shock you—she quit her job shortly thereafter, seeking a less-Bullish supervisor. Bulls are <u>great</u> on the basketball court, but <u>grate</u> at the workplace.

Communication with THEMs should not differ from communication with YOUs, in terms of its elements, only in terms of its intensity. Speaking the truth in love, attempting to resolve conflict, and intentional listening are principles for effective communication at any level. As we owe respect to all human beings, so we also owe appropriate and effective communication to all those THEMs in our lives with whom we inter-relate. With all due respect to former President Theodore Roosevelt, I have always been bothered by the expression, "Speak softly, and carry a big stick." I understand he was referring to America's place in the world order, but there is an underlying reference to clout, power, and intimidation. When it comes to effective communication, the playing field is even because it is built on relationships. I need to communicate with my THEMs as I would want THEMs to communicate with me.

Commitment

I can already hear you practicing your arguments on this one. How can I possibly commit anything or any part of myself to people with whom I have a distant or impersonal or superficial relationship, or no relationship at all? Isn't that a sort of oxymoron? Well, yes it is, if you regard commitment to THEMs in the same manner you regard commitment to YOUs. Personally, I don't. I believe very strongly that I have commitments to THEMs, whether or not I know them personally, and that I should hold tenaciously to my commitments. However, I also believe that these commitments are few in number and, as we mentioned earlier, can be summed up in what is known as the Golden Rule: Do unto THEMs as you would have THEMs do unto you. In other words, my true commitment is to a principle rather than to a person. This is real important to me, and let me explain why.

My commitment to my YOUs is based on my relationship with them. I love, adore, respect, enjoy, and highly regard them, or they would not be YOUs to me. Therefore, my commitment is based on a personal knowledge of them, as well as a sacred relationship. The same cannot be said for my THEMs. Some of them are wonderful human beings, and some go out of their way to do inhumane things to other human beings. Some are missionaries, and some are axe-murderers. Some devote their lives to helping others achieve success, and some devote their lives to ripping-off others. Some attempt to empower others, and some will stop at nothing to amass all power unto themselves. Some would become YOUs to me if I only knew them, and some would never let anyone get close enough to become a YOU.

What I am trying to say here is that, while I can base my commitment to YOUs on my personal relationship with them, I can only base my commitment to THEMs on a principle or value, because otherwise I will allow my tunnel vision to determine whether or not I can commit. As I relinquish my self-appointed position as Judge of the Universe (more on this in the next chapter), I realize that my personal standards of what constitutes acceptable behavior or acceptable people are flawed because I am imperfect, biased, prejudiced, and see things through my eyes only. Because of my imperfections and biases, I will have a tendency to regard some THEMs as equal human beings, while regarding other THEMs as less than equal, and this selection process will dictate how I wish to commit my respect to others.

My personal choice is to commit my respect to <u>all</u> human beings, based simply on the fact that they are people and, in my own belief system, created in the image of God. If I allow my personal code of conduct standards to influence my commitment of that respect, then I will heap commitment on some individuals, while withdrawing it from others. I will commit to respect the loving, caring, helpful, socially active, giving, and charitable people, while despising those who steal, maim, rape, kill, and cause damage to other people's lives.

Personally, I do not believe I have that right because I have resigned from being the Judge of the Universe. Who is to say that their actions are that much worse than things I have done which have injured other people? Who has set the bar at the perfect level so that I am due the commitment of respect and they are not? Who has determined that the normal curve is the standard by which we are evaluated, and that I have maintained a "B+" existence, while they have atrophied to a "D-" level? My imperfections disqualify me from being the ultimate evaluator of the worth-whileness of people, and so I choose to err on the side of commitment to a principle, which is to respect the personhood of all human individuals.

I hope this is making sense, and please do not think for one minute that I am condoning behavior which violates other human beings, or excusing cruel or violent acts which de-humanize people. I am not, and certainly the tone of this book would suggest that we all support behavior which is loving and gentle, and repudiate behavior which is less than that. The point I wish to emphasize is that I believe I owe the commitment of respect to all human beings, regardless of whether or not I know them, or agree with their positions, or share their values, or condone their behavior. <u>I choose to differentiate between the being and the behavior.</u>

So how does this flesh out in the real world? How do I go about committing my respect to the THEMs in my life? Let me suggest a couple of scenarios. First, with a co-worker or other professional colleague—I respect this person, not only as a human being, but as someone with whom I have a personal relationship. I know that this person has some special abilities or talents at the workplace, and is someone who is trying to succeed professionally, just as I am. I also realize that we will probably continue to work together, so it is in our best interest to maintain a positive and healthy relationship.

Although we may disagree at times, I will make an effort to always explain that my disagreement is not a personal issue, but a professional one. I will model my commitment to the relationship even if the other person fails to do the same. I will quietly, yet assertively, explain that I cannot communicate effectively unless there is mutual respect and adult-adult behavior. I will resist the temptation to fight fire with fire, which would prevent meaningful interaction in the future. To do otherwise would violate my commitment to be a professional employee, and respect other individuals.

Second, with a casual acquaintance—I respect this person as a human being, no better or worse than I am, with abilities, limitations, defects, potential, and aspirations. Therefore, I am committed to treating this person with respect and gentleness. If we are engaged in a meaningful conversation which is important enough to continue, I will make every attempt to maintain a mature level of discussion, not allowing it to deteriorate into personalizing or name-calling. If it becomes impossible for us to understand each other, or if the other person does not wish to play by the same rules, I will terminate the interchange, but I will do it with dignity, and I will not be seduced by the temptation to put the other person down, no matter how good it would make me feel for the moment. To do so would be to violate my commitment to respect other human beings.

Third, with someone I do not know, and probably will never meet—I respect this person as a human being, who is probably attempting to make the most out of his or her life, as I am. I recognize the fact that we are both imperfect people, struggling to "do" life in such a way as to achieve maximum satisfaction. As the good and bad experiences of my life have influenced the way I behave toward myself and others, I assume the same of this other person.

I will attempt not to judge this person based on my perceptions because I know that they emanate from my tunnel vision, and because I do not believe that this person has any right to judge me. I will maintain my respect for any human being, regardless of attitudes, values, beliefs, or behavior. I will not demean actions he or she may take just because I do not understand them or would choose not to adopt them as my own. I will recognize my place in society as a fellow human being, and not the authority figure who doles out judgment and criticism. I will respect the personhood of all human beings.

Let me conclude this chapter with one last reference to the Golden Rule. Many of us tend to read this as we <u>wish</u> it had been written instead of how it was really written. We like to edit it as follows: "Do unto THEMs (mentally) as you would like to do unto THEMs (physically) if you had the opportunity." This is called self-righteousness, and we will address it in more detail in the next chapter. For now, let's concentrate on the "Hit Me" aspect of dealing with the THEMs in our lives.

Is there a place for relationship-building with THEMs? Absolutely, and it can be a wonderfully eye-opening and growing experience, with opportunities for new friendships, or at least renewed understanding of others. Is there a place for communication with THEMs? Of course, and it can lead to effective interactions which are beneficial for all, and it can reveal marvelous unforeseen potential which would have been shrouded if people had not taken the risk to honestly communicate with each other. Is there a place for commitment with THEMs? I hope you can answer "yes" to this one because I sincerely believe that this is the culmination of Part 1 of this book—truly understanding yourself. I want to elaborate just a little on this because I feel so deeply that this is a crucial point.

Do unto those with whom you cannot agree as you would have them do unto you.

If you can absolutely not commit to respecting those with whom you disagree or do not share values, I would urge you to review the first three chapters of this book. At a tremendous risk to my credibility, I will boldly suggest that if you are unable to respect other human beings due to their attitudes or behaviors which are not in concert with your own, you do not understand yourself, or you do not like yourself, or you are not secure within yourself, or you have a greatly exaggerated view of yourself as Judge of the Universe.

This is an incredibly sensitive, yet extremely important, issue. If I wish to improve all my relationships, I must include the THEMs in my life. If I am pro-life, then I need to commit to respect the pro-choice THEMs, because they are as deeply committed to their cause as I am to mine. If I am pro-labor, then I need to commit to respect the pro-management THEMs, regardless of whether or not I agree with their positions. If I read about (which I did last month) a father who clubbed-to-death his five-year-old twins because they were tardy in their attempts to be ready for nursery school, can I commit to respect him as a human being? Gosh, that's a tough one, since I have twins who are so incredibly precious to me that I would do almost anything for them. But I have to return to my principle that he also is a human being. I cannot condone his action in any way, shape, or form, at any time, and it totally infuriates me that he could stoop to such a violent level. My human nature side demands retribution. He should sit in the electric chair, and I should be allowed to pull the lever—slowly.

But he is a person, and I do not pretend to know his background, mental state, frustration point, education level, parental training, or other personal problems. Does that excuse what he did? Of course not—he took two innocent lives. But I am not his ultimate accuser or judge, and I choose to commit myself to respect him as a human being. It is possible that he is going through more anguish than I could imagine in one thousand lifetimes. I have made hundreds of mistakes for which I felt incredible remorse later. Thankfully, none of them resulted in lasting guilt and, ironic as it might sound, thankfully I am not God, whose heart breaks with every human tragedy, and who ultimately is the Judge of the Universe. I choose not to apply for that job.

CHAPTER 11

◆◆◆

ON A SCALE OF 1 TO 10, YOU ARE A 3

"Judge not, lest you be judged."
The Bible

Have you ever driven behind someone who had a strange vanity license plate like "U GO SLOW" or "OUTA MY WAY" or "TOP DOG" or even "TUB RING?" I have, and do you know what my first thought often is? "How stupid! What kind of moron would pay extra money to have something idiotic on his license plate? First, he must be an extravert because no introvert would show-off like that. And second, the message isn't funny or cute or meaningful, just stupid." Have you ever had similar thoughts, or am I alone in my judgmental attitudes of what people choose to do with their money, cars, or sense of humor?

Why do we have this tendency to be critical or judgmental of others? And do you notice that it happens so much more frequently with THEMs than with YOUs? That may be due in part to the fact that there are so many more THEMs in the world than YOUs, but I think it also has to do with the impersonal relationships we have with THEMs. We are far more understanding of YOUs simply because of who they are and what they mean to us. THEMs, however, are an entirely different ball game. And since we have no overt responsibility to them, nor do we have to explain our actions or attitudes, they are fair game for our barbs, one-liners, criticism, disgust, and judgment.

I mentioned in the last chapter that the way we relate to THEMs brings us full circle to what we discussed in Chapter 1—how we view ourselves, and how we regard ourselves in terms of self-image. Most psychologists, both legitimate and armchair, agree that those of us who maintain a negative posture toward others suffer from a fairly serious dose of inferiority. Those of us who instantaneously detect the flaws in others, rather than the attributes, typically do not esteem ourselves very highly. I stress this because I believe it is an accurate indicator of my self-understanding. I can fool myself into thinking I know who I am, I can fool myself into thinking I know you, and I can even fool myself into thinking we have a splendid relationship, but if this last piece of the puzzle does not fit, then there is something wrong with the other pieces, and I need to begin the assessment process all over again.

Stay

The emphasis in the last chapter was on "HIT ME," the aggressive action steps of building relationships with THEMs, communicating with them, and commiting to them in an appropriate manner. Now I would like to focus on the "STAY" side of the equation, where I need to pull back and remain inactive, electing not to proceed with what may be a natural course of action for me. In this regard, I want to concentrate on two words, although I use them interchangeably and consider them to be one concept: **criticism** and **judgment.** The question I would pose is, "How can I become more understanding and accepting of the opinions and actions of others, and less critical and judgmental, especially with people whose lives I have not lived and whose experiences are unknown to me?" Sounds like a tall order, doesn't it?

I would suggest there is a very important issue here to be explained and understood. In my opinion, we need to make a clear distinction between judgment of: a) the behavior of others which is illegal, socially unacceptable, or violent to innocent people, and b) the behavior which I tend to judge because it is not in concert with my personal values, choices, or whims.

As citizens of the human race, we have a duty to pronounce judgment on behavior which threatens or does damage to unsuspecting or innocent people, particularly children or those unable to fend for themselves. To refrain from taking a moral stance on such issues is cowardly. I am going to assume that most of us agree with that premise, and so I wish to focus attention on the second part of the statement, which is judgment of the behavior of others which I do not support because of my personal values, choices, and whims. My contention is that I have a right to disagree with such behavior of others, but to criticize or judge the behavior or the person is to evidence a character flaw which reflects back on me.

"Here Come The Judge."
– Flip Wilson

Let me make a statement which is bound to get me in trouble with some people—most of our criticisms emanate from what I would call blatant arrogance. Notice I did not say <u>intentional</u> arrogance because I truly believe that we do not mean to come across that way. But if you step back from yourself and view the scenario objectively and impersonally (and this is a great deal easier for thinkers than it is for feelers), you will probably come to the conclusion that my criticism of another's behavior means that I am evaluating him or her according to my own standards. That is arrogance. It may be as trivial as ordering a dish from the menu, and someone else remarking, "Oh yuk, how can you stand that stuff?" Do you get the feeling that you ordered the wrong meal? Would you feel differently if the individual had said, "I personally don't like that dish, but I'm glad you found something that will taste good to you?"

Let's take an example that might be more meaningful. At work, you have to make a decision of contracting between Vendor A and Vendor B. You do your homework, but there is no clear-cut winner, so you just make a decision. A co-worker then states, "Bad idea. You made a wrong decision." Don't you get the feeling that there is some blatant arrogance lurking behind the retort? Doesn't the co-worker imply that his or her standards are loftier than your own, and therefore yours are inferior?

I cannot begin to tell you how many times I have heard parents debate about the "best" way to raise children or discipline them. I am ashamed to admit this, but when I taught elementary school (with a Masters degree in Elementary Education), I had all the answers, and freely shared them with friends who were parents. I remember some of them glaring at me and saying, "Wait till you have kids of your own." I didn't understand what the fuss was all about because I was a professional "kid raiser" with blatant arrogance.

Then I had children, and for the past almost 20 years, I have been quite guarded in what kinds of advice I offer to parents. I no longer insist that they meet my pinnacle of success standards. It may sound ironic, but I have become a lot smarter by realizing that I am not as smart as I once thought I was. Socrates once lectured his Athenian accusers (paraphrase): "You think that you are wise, but you are not. I know that I am not wise, therefore I am wiser than you." For that, he was forced to drink hemlock, so be sure that you do not carry this anti-arrogance thing too far.

Because such arrogance can be real subtle, and because most of us recognize it in others but not in ourselves, let me offer you a few scenarios to consider. Can you identify with any of them? Mentally check off the ones that apply.

✓ When someone passes me on the highway, he is reckless and driving too fast; when I am trying to pass someone, he is a nuisance and driving too slowly. My driving speed is the correct one.

✓ People who are more witty and clever than I am are shallow and devoid of maturity; people who are less witty and clever are dull, boring, and uninspiring. My sense of humor is the correct one.

✓ If my neighbor owns a Doberman and I own a cockatoo, my neighbor is a brute; if I own a Doberman and he owns a cockatoo, then he is a wimp. My choice of pets is the correct one.

✓ People who work more hours than I do are workaholics and have no life; people who work fewer hours than I do are not loyal to the company and have no initiative. My work hours are the correct ones.

✓ If someone drinks one more beer than I do, he is an alcoholic; if he drinks one less beer than I do, he is anti-social or not really a man. My choice of alcohol consumption is the correct one.

✓ If someone wears yellow when I wear black, she is eccentric and seeking attention; if she wears black when I wear yellow, she is drab, uninteresting, and stylishly challenged. My choice of wardrobe is the correct one.

✓ People who live in a neighborhood which is more up-scale than my neighborhood are haughty, pretentious, and elitist; people who live in a neighborhood which is less up-scale than my neighborhood are unsuccessful, shiftless, and lazy. My choice of neighborhoods is the correct one.

None of us would admit to consciously judging others according to the above criteria, but I hear comments every day that indicate otherwise. When was the last time you saw someone on TV and announced, "That is a horrible tie (or sweater or dress)?" Follow-up that assertion with the question, "According to whose standards?"

Let me take the temptation to be the Judge of the Universe a tragic step further because this is where it becomes insidious, cruel, vicious, slanderous, and evil. When we make up our minds that certain people do not measure up to our perfect standards of conduct, we have a tendency to write them off. At that point, we view everything they do or say with a jaundiced and critical eye. Every day is an audition, and they have to continuously prove themselves. They are guilty until proven innocent.

There is a further tendency to then assume additional vile behavior or atrocities. In other words, they cannot win. The damning label has been affixed, and it will never be removed. In my mind, this causes two problems, in addition to the one mentioned in the previous chapter, that all human beings are worthy of respect due to their personhood. First, it demonstrates an alarming degree of unforgiving spite, which is unhealthy, at best. Second, it prevents us from the possibility of experiencing learning opportunities because of the barriers we have erected. A very wise man, who is also a friend of mine, once shared with me, "The more critical I am of other people, the more I discover that it limits my ability to learn from them." How true. It is a sad day when I cannot accept truth or growth statements from certain people because I have chosen to dismiss them as inferior individuals who do not measure up to my standards of behavior.

> *"The more critical I am of other people,*
> *the more I discover that it limits*
> *my ability to learn from them."*
> *– Dr. William Owen*

How would you like to be remembered for the worst thing you ever did in your life? Pretty scary, isn't it? In my case, they would have several dozen to choose from. And yet, we sometimes tend to do that. Think about a public figure (politics, sports, entertainment) who you have been judgmental of in the past. What do you remember best about him or her?

How would you describe the person to someone who had never heard of him or her? How fair would you be in your assessment? What would you emphasize?

Take just a minute right now to evaluate yourself in this regard. As you consider people in general (THEMs), do you lean more toward acceptance, positive feelings, and understanding, or do you tend to find fault, have negative feelings, and detect dirt? When a story breaks in the newspapers about someone who has been accused of a crime or an indiscretion, is your tendency to think, "Let's check the facts to determine guilt or innocence," or is your tendency to react, "Let's nail the *&#@*!" This can be a helpful exercise, but only if we are truly honest in our self-appraisals. If I am honestly seeking to become a better person with regard to my relationships with others, then I need to know where my weak spots are. Once I have identified them and determined that I wish to correct them and improve myself, then I am well on the road to recovery.

Assumptions

From my experience, I have learned that many of our judgmental attitudes arise from (in addition to arrogance, and definitely connected to it) assumptions we make of people, their lives, attitudes, values, goals and ambitions, opinions, and intentions. We have already determined that to assume is risky, at best, and unfortunately, most of our assumptions of our THEMs are inaccurate because they are based on knowledge we do not have about people we do not know. But somehow we form these assumptions and cling to them tenaciously, perhaps because the security of an assumption is more comforting than the insecurity of not knowing.

Have you ever heard someone say (or have you ever said yourself), "I just <u>know</u> what they are thinking?" That is very impressive, and there is a great deal of money to be made if the talent is really there, but it probably isn't. How about this scenario: You invite someone to go to lunch with you and several other people, and the person politely declines. What is your response (internally)? Do you give the person the benefit of the doubt, or do you assume that you were snubbed, and vow never again to ask him or her to share a meal? In every human encounter which raises questions, we have the choice to assume the best or the worst about the other person. Which is your tendency?

Last year, I had a player on the high school baseball team which I manage who was less than a role model. He had several unpleasant encounters with umpires, constantly forgot to look at me for signs when he was batting, and almost got into an ugly fight with an opposing player. As a manager, I learned that he was not terribly reliable, and he was a contributing cause to my ever-graying hair. About halfway into the season, he informed me that he would miss about four games because he was going on vacation with his father, but he promised that he would be at the park for our Friday night game.

I had him in the line-up for the Friday game, but he did not show up, nor was he there for the Saturday, Sunday, or Monday games. He did not call me, and I had no idea where he was. Needless to say, I was infuriated, as I had instructed all the players to notify me if they would miss a game. I must confess that inwardly I assumed he had blown off the team, that I might never see him again, and I did not place him in the line-up for the next game. In fact, I had a speech prepared that would have impressed General Patton. Something (perhaps a slight unexpected twinge of wisdom) told me to keep my assumptions to myself, and to give him a break and think the best about him until I was proven wrong. So I chose not to bad-mouth him in front of the rest of the team.

At our next game, the following Thursday, he showed up, and I pulled him aside, prepared to reconfigure his anatomy with my diatribe. At that point, he explained to me that he had been in a hospital in Wyoming with a problem which I discovered later was actually life-threatening (his immune system had broken down, and could not absorb the anti-bodies). In that condition, it had not occurred to him to call me. Obviously, I never got to deliver my speech, but here is the critical lesson which was reinforced to me—<u>even in the face of past experiences which would seem to justify negative assumptions, hold your fire</u>. Assume the best, and take your chances with the rest. Once again I was reminded of a commitment I have made many times over—give them a break. If I am going to be wrong, I would rather be wrong assuming the best of others than assuming the worst of others. I realize there are dangers here. I may be devastated, I may be hurt, I may be very wrong, I may look naïve and stupid, but all that is worth it to me if I do not offend an innocent person, nor unfairly judge someone else according to my imperfect standards.

In Chapter 1, I wrote about the person who does not understand him or her self, but attempts to understand others and pass judgment on their behavior. Here is where I come full-circle. I have found in my life that the more I truly understand myself, the more I appreciate the goodness of others. The better I see myself for who I really am, with all my warts, blemishes, and imperfections, the more tolerant I am of others who struggle just like I do. The more I focus on how I have been blessed in my life, and how undeserving I am of my extremely fortunate circumstances, the more gracious I tend to be toward others, and the less judgmental I am of their attitudes and behavior.

This is so easy to talk about and, in a cognitive way, it makes absolute sense, but in the heat of the moment, many of us fail to follow through on our desires to be more understanding and less critical and judgmental. It is so easy to fall prey to the temptation to assume that someone else is wrong or stupid. Because I do not know the background or life experiences of most of the THEMs in my life, I have a tendency to don my tunnel vision glasses, evaluate them according to my personal standards, and once again claim the throne as Judge of the Universe. What can I do about this tendency? As I reflect on this, the word that comes to mind is humility.

Humility

Let me share my definition of the word humility, which may or may not be the same as your own definition. Webster refers to it with synonyms such as submission, courtesy, lowliness, and meekness. Interestingly, he also calls it "freedom from arrogance," which I have associated with a critical spirit. I have no problem with Webster's synonyms, but I would like to offer a slightly different slant on what humility is. I believe humility is having an accurate picture of who I am, not thinking too highly of myself, nor too lowly. We often think a humble person is one who never takes credit for anything, who demeans him or her self, or who takes great pains to remain in the background in an effort to deflect praise or adoration. Let's not confuse true humility with false humility.

Often after a televised professional athletic game, the announcers or commentators will name a "Most Valuable Player" for the game (a pet peeve of mine, in case you are interested. During the entire game, they emphasize teamwork, and then at the game's conclusion, they select one person as the "star" of the game. I need to be less critical and judgmental of their obvious stupidity—darn it, why can't they be perfect like me?). The humble athlete will neither shrink from the attention, nor bask in it, but rather express gratitude that he or she has been blessed with talent, and emphasize that it was a "team victory," often mentioning certain teammates by name for their contributions.

I believe a humble person is one who recognizes both his or her strengths and weaknesses, does not attempt to hide either one, and is comfortable talking about both in a non-boastful or arrogant way. Let me illustrate. In a world of thousands of effective leaders, two stand out in my mind because of their humility. The first is Michael Jordan (a name you recognize) and the second is my minister (whose name you probably would <u>not</u> recognize, although he started a church about 25 years ago which may well be the largest and most influential on the planet). Both men unashamedly and with confidence refer to themselves as leaders, accepting the role with all of its rewards and responsibilities, not boasting or lording their abilities over those of other people, but realistically assessing their gifts and talents, and also recognizing the strengths of others which complement their own.

When I think of humility as having the realistic picture of who I am, it certainly assists me in being more thoughtful, patient, kind, considerate, and accepting toward others, and far less critical and judgmental, because we are all on a level playing field. I may be smarter than some, but not as smart as others. I may be wealthier than some, but not as wealthy as others. I may have more talents than some, but not as many talents as others.

Above all, I am a person just like everyone else is, a person with dreams and goals, fears and trepidation, loved ones, beliefs, precious possessions, friends, and desires to achieve and succeed. In that context, who am I to appoint myself as Judge of the Universe? Who am I to criticize you because you have different ideas or ways of doing things? Who am I to label you because you do not measure up to my self-selected standards? Who am I to <u>ever</u> judge another human being because he or she chooses to have values and ambitions and habits which vary from my own? True humility can be a powerful force in assisting us in the exercise of cleansing our souls from critical thinking and judgmental damning.

Let me reemphasize that there is a legitimate place for constructive criticism, assessment, and evaluation, particularly in a supervisor-supervisee relationship at the work place. I am certainly not advocating that no one is ever in a position to correct another, or to hold that individual to certain standards. But we are talking here about criticism and judgment which we place upon another person because his or her behavior, attitudes, or opinions conflict with our own values, choices, and whims. It is in that arena that I am strongly suggesting we have no right to assume judicial authority.

I am acutely aware that some of you reading this book will disagree with me from time to time regarding what I have written (although I assume that by the time you are this far, you either have benefited from the content, or you are amassing an arsenal of rebuttal, and are becoming angrier by the minute). In either case, please allow me to reassure you that my expressed ideas about criticism and judgment are not mere words, but concepts which I have thought about and wrestled with for many years. In other words, while I feel strongly about what I have written, I choose not to criticize or judge anyone who opposes my views and beliefs.

These are my opinions. They are well-thought-out, and based on many years of experience, but I do not pretend to be the ultimate authority on relationships, nor do I fantasize about having a corner on truth. I do not claim to be the Chicago-area distributor of wisdom. As I have mentioned before, I am a fellow-struggler in life. I continue to make mistakes which frustrate me, although I am getting better about learning from them, and I tend to make fewer of them than I used to. Several years ago, I coined an expression (actually I added to an already well-known expression). It goes like this: "To err is human. To err repeatedly is stupid." My goal is to continue to learn and to grow, and part of that process is to accept disagreement without retaliation, and in fact, to learn from it.

I do confess to having certain assumptions about anyone reading this book. My guess is that you are a continuous seeker of self-improvement, or you would not have stayed with me for 11 chapters. In that regard I salute you, and I trust that at least several of the things I have mentioned in the book have been helpful in your quest toward becoming a more relational person. The point I wish to emphasize is that we do not have to agree on everything in order to be mutually respectful toward each other. I choose not to criticize or judge those who have questions or objections to what I have written, and I trust you will also respect my beliefs and personhood.

Where Do I Go From Here?

I am going to make the bold assumption at this point that most of us would like to be more understanding and accepting of others, and less critical and judgmental of their attitudes and behaviors which we don't understand. So how do we go about doing it? What is the magical formula?

Surprise! There is no formula or blueprint or flow chart. But I do have five ideas which have been helpful to me, and I wish to share them to see if you might benefit also. I do not claim that they are exhaustive or foolproof, but I offer them as suggestions which I have used, and they have served me well. Here is my pentagon of judgment-busting activities.

1. Check It Out Before You Write It Off

As I have previously stated, I believe that many of our criticisms surface because of assumptions we make which may or may not be true. Unfortunately, perception is reality. Have you ever met someone who you had already decided you were not going to like, possibly because of something you had heard about him or her? Or have you ever attended a play or movie, under duress or out of obligation, knowing full well that you were going to hate it? How open-minded or objective were you after having those preconceived notions? Were you able to learn anything new or benefit in any way from the experience or the introduction?

I tend to do this with TV sit-coms, which I typically dismiss out of hand as frivolous, mindless, and a colossal waste of time (an admitted arrogant bias on my part). Because of my prejudice, I do not watch such shows. There are occasions, however, when I am forced to view a sit-com, in order to not be rude to another person, or offend him or her. I confess that I convince myself beforehand that there will be nothing humorous or worthwhile about the show, and I mentally tune out for 30 minutes. How much better would I serve myself if I said something like this: "This is not my first choice, but I'm stuck here for the next half hour. I will watch the show carefully, and attempt to pick up at least one thing which might be beneficial, even if it is just a little bit of relaxing levity. I will check out the show's content before writing it off."

If this works with something as trivial as a TV show, how much more benefit might it have with an encounter with a human being? Recall my story in the last chapter about the baseball manager who I had assumed was distant, aloof, and a bit conceited. If I had pursued my gut feelings to write him off before checking out what he was really like, I would have missed a wonderful opportunity. I would urge you to commit to yourself to refrain from writing off people or things because of preconceived comments or opinions, but rather check them out objectively and curiously to see what you might gain from them.

2. Give Them A Break

When I was a kid, there was an expression I learned that went like this: "You can't judge a book by its cover." In some ways, this is similar to checking it out before writing it off, but it goes one step further. It assumes that you have already completed the task of checking out, and you still have a hard time accepting the person, or idea, or behavior. The tendency is still there to criticize or judge, and in fact maybe it is stronger than it was previously.

First let me suggest that possibly the criticism is legitimate, and you would be better off to cut your losses and not pursue the relationship. Take the TV sit-com example again. After I have watched the show once or twice, honestly attempting to withhold criticism, I determine that it is indeed frivolous, mindless, and a colossal waste of time. At that point, I will write it off in my mind because it conflicts with my values or choices, but then I need to be very careful not to criticize or judge others who may enjoy the show and find it to be outrageously funny. I have the right to not enjoy a TV show, but I choose not to label other TV watchers according to my personal standards.

With regard to meeting someone about whom you may have a preconceived negative perception, I would encourage you to insist on witnessing the negative behavior first-hand before succumbing to the temptation of assuming its existence. Refer back to Chapter 6 for some practical ideas on how to STOP making assumptions, and intentionally seek contrary evidence.

One year when I taught sixth grade, I had a student named Billy. He was a really cute kid, and very bright (I just found out about a year ago that he is a medical doctor, and doing quite well). He was also charming, and very popular with other teachers and fellow students. But he had one mannerism that used to irritate the heck out of me. When he was being reprimanded for something (which wasn't often), he would smirk, and that drove me absolutely crazy. Do you remember when your mother or a teacher would say to you, "Wipe that smirk off your face before I have to?" That was how I felt about Billy on those occasions. I just wanted to take his cute little face and twist it into next week.

Then one day I had a long discussion with Billy's mom, and what she told me went something like this: "When Billy gets embarrassed, he smirks. That is his defense mechanism. Please don't think he is being disrespectful. He is actually mortified, and that is the way he reacts to his embarrassment." I had no problem believing that because he was such a neat kid in every other way. So I learned a lesson, which I have relived many times over the years. When I don't understand the way people look, react, or behave, give them a break. Assume the best until proven wrong. If I truly believe that the majority of people are good and not evil, and I do, then I am best served by cutting them some slack, and not making erroneous assumptions for which I must apologize later.

3. Focus On The Best In People, Not The Worst

We have a sick tendency in our society to utterly bask in the glow of watching people fail. That is one of the reasons why tabloids are so popular. Some people just love to see others exposed for an indiscretion or wrongdoing, even if it turns out to be untrue. There is something about the human spirit that thrives on lurking around others, waiting to see them make that one mistake so we can pounce on them. I would call this the Vulture Syndrome. Warren Bennis, a management guru and author of several books on leadership, labels it "manure detecting" (not exactly his words, but close enough). It is the art of sifting through thousands of behaviors in a person's life until we discover one which might cause that individual some embarrassment, and then exploiting it. Among historians, Richard Nixon's legacy will be that he was possibly the most successful foreign policy President in American history, but for the rest of the millions of citizens who were alive in the 60s and 70s, he will forever be linked with Watergate.

There is a children's board game which has been around forever, and it is called "Chutes and Ladders." I played it as a kid, I played it with my own boys, and I can't wait for them to have children of their own so I can play it some more. The idea of the game is that you attempt to get from square one to square one hundred by rolling dice. The first one to square one hundred is the winner.

If you get lucky, you land on a space which has a ladder, which means you can advance a number of spaces all at once. On the other hand, if you are not so lucky, you can land on a space which has a chute. That means you go back 20 or 30 spaces, or possibly back to square one. In fact, if I recall correctly, there is a space near the finish line which has a chute that will drop you back to the very beginning. That is <u>very</u> unlucky, but I remember landing on it from time to time.

The metaphor here is obvious, at least to me. You can plod and plod for years to attain your goal, but one mistake can possibly sink your boat. One indiscretion, one misjudgment, one slip-up can destroy a life-time of honorable effort and achievement. We tend to be unforgiving people who prefer to remember the worst over the best.

Stop for just a moment and think about this: is there someone who you would love to see fail, or be publicly humiliated? Who would that be? The President of the United States, or another prominent politician? A professional athlete? A movie star? Your boss? I would bet I hit a sore spot there, and I would like to see a show of hands on that one. How many of you would be unspeakably gleeful if your boss were to fall into disrepute? In fact, how many of you have actually conjured up mental images of how to make that happen?

For over 50 years, the Reverend Billy Graham has been the most celebrated and significant and widely known religious leader in the world. He has had countless opportunities to make a mistake that would prove fatal to his person and his ministry. In the wake of tele-evangelists dropping like flies for moral failures, Dr. Graham has remained unblemished for one-half century. But I would bet my life that there are reporters and skeptics and cynics who prayed (ironic, isn't it?) for the day when he would make the mistake that they could chronicle to the world, discrediting him, and attempting to overshadow the mission of the man, which profoundly affected millions of lives across the globe.

After you have answered the question I asked two paragraphs ago, ask yourself this one: "Would I like people to remember me for the worst moment of my life?" If you answer "yes" to that, please seek help immediately. Think about this scenario for a moment—you have been a loyal employee for many years, often working more hours than were required, offering suggestions which benefited the company, and pouring your soul into achieving success for the good of the organization. Then one day, you make a mistake or an unfortunate decision, probably not even a serious one. Suddenly you are labeled as the "screw up." How do you feel about that? In the overall scheme of things at work over several decades, is it right that people remember you for your error?

You old-time football fans will remember this. In the 60s, the Minnesota Vikings had a defensive line, unparalleled in the NFL, which became known as the Purple People Eaters. Quarterbacks around the league quaked when they realized that their next opponent was Minnesota, and many of them consulted their attorneys for the current status of their wills and life insurance policies. One of the four Purple People Eaters, Jim Marshall, was a phenomenal pass rusher, as were his trio of intimidators. Marshall made numerous sacks and interceptions, but one day he became turned around on an interception, and he ran toward his own end zone, where he was tackled for a safety. In spite of the hundreds of contributions he made to his team over many years, would you like to guess what his nickname is to knowledgeable football fans everywhere? "Wrong Way Marshall."

How would you like to be remembered for the worst moment of your life? I wouldn't. My guess is you wouldn't either, and I suggest that one way to accelerate judgment-busting is to focus on the best features of people, not the worst.

4. Keep Your Criticism Current

The Academic Dean of a college where I once taught used this expression, and I have incorporated it into my psyche ever since. It has helped me enormously in my relationships with others. Because a person makes a mistake on one occasion, or even develops a pattern of behavior with which I cannot agree or stomach, that does not mean that he or she will forever adopt the same stance. Wonder of wonders—people do change with time and maturity, sometimes for the better. As I would not want to be remembered for the worst moment in my life, I also would not want to be remembered for the kind of person I may have been at one point in my life. I shared with you earlier that before I had children of my own, I had all the answers to child rearing due to my educational background. Piece of cake—follow the theories, kids develop perfectly.

If I were to interact today with those people who I lectured on how to raise their children, would I want them to remember me as the arrogant know-it-all perfect father? Gosh, I hope not. Just last night, I was teaching a class on relationships between parents and children, and one of my adult students praised me for how I have put theory into practice, treating my own sons (since infancy) as real people and mature human beings instead of enforcing my power and control over helpless "property." Of course, she will receive an "A" in the course for her astute perceptions, but if only she knew the truth about how many times I have failed in my efforts. As a life-long learner, I don't want people to criticize me for the way I used to be. I want them to witness my growth, celebrate my learnings, and evaluate me on where I am today, not yesterday. I want people to keep their criticism current when they judge who I am as a person.

For those of you who recently attended a high school reunion (10th year, 20th year, 30th year), have your perceptions about your classmates altered? Have you discovered that those who were most self-assured in high school have joined the rest of us normal folks? Have you observed that those who were the most "clique-ish" in high school have mellowed and are more accepting of us regular people? Have you realized that the ones voted "most likely to end up in jail or on skid row" are the people who discovered their niche, put it all together, and are impressively successful? People change with age and maturity, and we owe it to ourselves and to them to keep our criticisms current.

I heard a story the other day about a man who was a white supremacist in the South in the 60s. He and several friends ventured out one day to attack civil rights workers, with the intent to murder them. Their plans were foiled, and he landed in prison. While there, he turned his life around, and after he was paroled, he exerted the same vigor he had once drawn upon for hatred, to establish a haven for people of all races. Today, he is the minister of a large multi-racial church, where he espouses love, respect, concern, and equal treatment for all people. How would you feel if you were one of his parish members or his friend, and someone referred to him as "that racist pig, who should rot in his grave?" A way to bust judgment-thinking is to keep your criticism current.

5. Walk A Mile In My Moccasins

This famous Indian proverb is so well-known that we tend to gloss over its incredible significance as a life motto in the process of judgment-busting. As I stated in the very first chapter, how can I know what it is like to go through life as a blind person, or someone of a different race or gender? I cannot, but I certainly can be quick to find their faults and criticize their behavior. It takes a conscious effort to pause and ask myself what it might be like to actually be that other person.

Sometimes I become frustrated with my adult students when they are late to class, only to realize later that after working eight hours that day, they had to take public transportation to school, had no time for dinner, and are both exhausted and hungry. And I expect them to give me their best effort for the next four hours? Or I get irritated because the paper that was due in class tonight did not get completed on time. My first reaction is, "You had two weeks to finish the paper. Why isn't it done?"

And then I discover that in addition to working every day, the student cares for her four children because she is a single mom, she does extra work on the side to help make ends meet, she tends to a very ill aunt, she pays someone else to type her papers because she cannot afford a word processor, and her typist lost the entire document due to a computer crash. I am not making excuses for students who do not exert the proper effort or follow-through on their assignments. What I am saying is that I do not know what it is like to be someone else, and before I smugly don my judge's robe, I need to take a hard look at the reality of who that other person is.

An athlete loses his cool at a press conference and lashes out at the reporters, storming out of the room. Many people are quick to denounce him, reasoning that with his extravagant salary and fame, he should be under control at all times, and there is no excuse for him acting that way in public. How many of us take the time to ask questions like: I wonder what it is like to be that person? What is it like to be that well-known? What is it like to be under the microscope all the time? What is it like to be unable to go out in public without being mobbed and asked for favors and autographs?

With apologies to sports reporters who are just doing their jobs, what is it like to be asked the same inane questions night after night? "So how does it feel to lose that playoff game by one point? Are you disappointed?" If someone asked me that question, I would probably want to rearrange his face. Isaiah Thomas, who played professional basketball for a number of years, and then was the general manager for another pro team, was asked about the attitude of one of his players, who appeared to be cocky, brazen, and not much of a gentleman. Thomas' response went something like this: "If you knew the neighborhood where he grew up, if he were not cocky and brazen, and were more of a gentleman, he would not even be alive today. He would not have survived his childhood." Walk a mile in my moccasins.

A friend of mine has said to me on numerous occasions, "You couldn't do my job for a week. You would quit. You have no idea what it is like to do what I do." That is probably correct. How often we think that other people have it so much easier than we do. How quick we are to criticize and judge their attitudes and behavior. How easy it is for us to play Judge of the Universe without having been where the "accused" has been. As Jesus responded to the "judges" who were about to stone to death the woman taken in adultery, "Let you who is without sin cast the first stone."

The Microscope And The Mirror

I have found in my life that taking on the role of a critic and judge eases the pain of having to look deeply into my soul to detect my own faults. The more I can focus on the faults of others, the less time and motivation I have to see my own shortcomings. If I can accuse someone of being haughty, then I can feel better because I don't need to recognize my own pride. If I can identify someone who is worthy of criticism because he or she treats people disrespectfully, then I have less time to evaluate how I interact with others. Certainly I cannot be as bad as he or she is. Having a microscope is a lot more comforting than having a mirror. Being a hammer is a lot more fun than being a nail.

Have you ever worked in an organization where problems were "fixed" by finding someone to blame them on? I have, and it would be comical if it were not so serious. I have sat in meetings where crucial problems were discussed, and as soon as the group decided who the "culprit" was, the issue was dismissed, and the meeting continued without discussion of how to solve the problem. At first I was flabbergasted, but over time I began to realize that this was the accepted way of dealing with problems. Use the microscope instead of the mirror and proceed to the next agenda item. Is it any wonder that the same problems existed in this organization year after year after year?

In closing this chapter, let me make one final comment because I believe it is absolutely imperative when it comes to judgment-busting. A critical or judgmental spirit does not die of natural causes. It must be put to death through a focused and concentrated effort, and a commitment to be accepting and appreciative of the THEMs in my life. You have heard the expression, "Time heals all wounds." Well, time does not heal all critical spirits. They are healed only by my intense resolve to vacate my position as Judge of the Universe. Anatomically speaking, my heart is larger than my mouth. I want that to be true in my behavior also.

Below, I have listed the names of several individuals who had outstanding and successful careers in their various fields, but who will probably be remembered by the general population for one major mistake. I hope that is not true, but I think I know better. On the blank line below, write your own name and ask yourself these questions. What is the worst thing I have ever done in my life? What is the greatest mistake I have ever made? Is that what I would like people to remember me for?

Wilber Mills
Pete Rose
Michael Milken
O.J. Simpson
Ted Kennedy
Marv Albert
Bill Clinton

CHAPTER 12

◆◆◆

WHO IS MY NEIGHBOR?

**"I had three chairs in my house:
one for solitude, two for
friendship, three for society."
– Henry David Thoreau
(quoted in _Familiar Quotations_, p. 683)**

Most of us are at least tangentially familiar with the biblical saga of the Good Samaritan. A man was walking down the road when he was abducted by thieves, who robbed him and beat him, and left him for dead. Two passers-by, a priest and a Levite (both religious figures), saw the victim, and chose to cross over to the other side of the road in order to avoid becoming involved. Then along came a Samaritan (a hated Samaritan). You must remember that the Jews and the Samaritans were bitter enemies (the Hatfields and the McCoys, only more vicious). But this Samaritan felt compassion for the innocent traveler, and so he bandaged up his wounds, put him on his own "beast" (probably a mule), escorted him to an inn, stayed with him that night, paid the lodging expense, and told the inn-keeper to maintain a record of the man's expenses, which he (the Samaritan) would pay in full on his return trip.

In other words, this guy gave the poor fellow a full ride. He took care of him physically, economically, and emotionally. Only Ed McMahon, appearing with a sweepstakes check of $10,000 million, could possibly have surprised the injured man more. My guess is that when the victim saw the Samaritan approaching, he thought, "Oh well, it doesn't get any worse than this. They already have my money, I'm bleeding to death, and I am powerless to defend myself against any further attack. This man will probably pour salt on my wounds, laugh in my face, and say, 'Adios sucker.' This is turning out to be a very bad day."

Imagine his shock when the long-time rival Samaritan showed pity on a fellow human being in distress. Imagine his anxious surprise when the Samaritan knelt beside him, washed the blood away, applied ointment and bandages (a well-supplied medic of a Samaritan), and loaded him on his own mule. Imagine his further astonishment when the Samaritan delivered him to an inn, bought a room for him, and offered to stay for the night to make sure he was all right. Imagine his consternation when the Samaritan announced the next morning that he was leaving on business, but that the injured man was to remain in the inn until he was completely healed, and that the hotel bill would be covered in full. Imagine his ultimate embarrassment when he recalled that he had been taught his entire life that all Samaritans were pond scum.

Who would you do that for? A loved one? A relative? A friend? An associate? A stranger? An enemy? For whom would you sacrifice your time, your money, and possibly your pride? In a world of billions and billions of people, who is my neighbor?

Of course, each of us needs to answer that question individually, but I would offer one personal response. My neighbor is anyone who I have the opportunity to influence or affect, either positively or negatively. As the Samaritan approached the wounded Jewish man, he could have walked by like the others did, he could have spit on him, he could have used an ethnic slur to insult him, or he even could have said, "I see that you are injured. I hope you feel better soon. Have a nice day." Not possessing a cellular phone to call 911, he could have proceeded to the inn and told the innkeeper about the injured man, who most likely would have been dead by the time help arrived. Or he could have elected to use whatever resources were available to him to assist in helping the one who needed help, which is what he did. In any case, the helpless man was his neighbor because the Samaritan was in a position to influence and affect, either positively or negatively.

> ### *My neighbor is anyone who I have the opportunity to influence or affect, either positively or negatively.*

If you can live with my definition for a few minutes, try to think who your neighbors are on any given day. Here are some suggestions:

✓ your co-workers
✓ the food server where you eat lunch
✓ your taxi cab driver
✓ the couple who own the cleaners where you pick up your shirts
  or blouses
✓ the person sitting next to you on the bus
✓ the man who shines your shoes
✓ the pedestrian walking in front of your car when you are in a hurry
✓ the salesperson who calls you on the phone
✓ the flight attendant who requests that you put up your tray table
✓ the homeless person who asks you for some money
✓ the grocery store clerk
✓ your hair dresser
✓ the person who cuts you off in traffic
✓ the referee at your daughter's soccer game
✓ the librarian who checks out your books
✓ the gas station attendant
✓ your personal banker
✓ the UPS person who rings your bell to deliver a special package
✓ the person in front of you at the express checkout counter who has
  more than 10 items
✓ the drive-up person who gives you a hot dog when you specifically
  requested a polish
✓ the desk clerk at the motel who informs you your room is not
  ready yet
✓ the mechanic who tells you it's time for a new automobile
✓ the nurse who misses your vein on the first two attempts
✓ the engineer of the 120-car freight train who waves as he passes by
✓ the management negotiator, when you represent labor
✓ the labor negotiator, when you represent management
✓ the boss who reprimands you unfairly
✓ the baggage claim representative who informs you they lost
  your luggage
✓ the snowplow driver who dumps 12 inches of dirty snow at the end of
  your driveway
✓ the pokey driver when you are in a hurry
✓ the person who requests a donation to a worthwhile charity
✓ your apartment next-door person who plays his music for the entire
  town to hear
✓ your condo-owner landlord who tells you he is selling the unit
✓ the person who backs into your car in the strip-mall parking lot

Had enough, or would you like to add several dozen of your own? These are our neighbors, and we have the opportunity to initiate a conversation with them, or respond to them in a manner that could be either positive or negative.

True story—While I was typing this list, the phone rang, and it was a lady attempting to sell me a subscription to a Chicago newspaper. Since I was concentrating on who my neighbor is, I naturally had to be as loving and polite as possible. I actually felt guilty declining the offer. I thanked her for calling and thinking about me, and I wished her well in her other calls for the rest of the day. I thought about telling her that she was beautiful, that I would love to send her flowers and take her to dinner, and that I would be delighted to put her kids through college, but I decided that might be more than she could handle from a stranger on a Monday morning.

In all seriousness, allow me one addendum to this scenario. We all have had telephone sales people who become rather obnoxious after we turn down their initial offer. They say things like, "Tell me why you don't want to accept this." At that point, we feel challenged (defensive) and want to react in like manner. We want to hang up or retort as vociferously as we can or belittle the person. I would like to think that this is a person who is trying to do his or her job, and while this individual may not have the interpersonal skills which are desirable to continuing a dialogue, I do not want to lower myself to his or her level. Instead, I will typically reply, "I told you I am not interested, and I do not owe you any explanation. Thank you for calling. Goodbye." And then I will hang up. Usually, the person will not hear my entire verbal masterpiece because he or she hangs up in the middle, but I feel good about the fact that I attempted to be kind and friendly, yet firm. I refused to discount or negate his or her personhood. Incidentally, it also makes me grateful for the jobs that I do not have.

> *"It's a beautiful day in the neighborhood,*
> *a beautiful day for a neighbor,*
> *would you be mine?"*
> *– Mr. (Fred) Rogers*

If my neighbor is anyone who I have the opportunity to influence or affect, either positively or negatively, then what responsibility do I have toward him or her? What do I owe the person, if anything? My response to that is clearly unremarkable and simple. In any interchange or situation with a neighbor, mentally change places with the individual so that you become him or her for the moment, and he or she becomes you. Then interact with the person as you would want that individual to interact with you or with a loved one of yours. Sounds a lot like the Golden Rule, doesn't it? But maybe it will come more alive if we rename it the Relationship Rule.

The Relationship Rule

In any given encounter with someone who I have the opportunity to influence or affect, either positively or negatively, I will speak to and act toward him or her as I would want that person to speak to and act toward me. Do you remember two chapters back when I related the story of a former supervisor who reprimanded a co-worker of mine by exploding, "You get two mistakes with me, and you already have made your first one?" If he had considered the Relationship Rule for a minute before confronting her, would he have used the same approach? Probably not, because he didn't like it when people attempted to intimidate him. So why did he do it to someone else?

The next time you pick up your cleaning and there is a snafu, what might be a way to problem-solve without treating the clerk or owner in a way that you would not want to be treated? The next time you get into a dispute with someone at work over an issue which is important to both of you, what might be a way to discover a win-win solution while dealing personally with the fellow employee in a way that you also would like to be handled? I was at a basketball game once where, during a time-out, a man stood up to stretch. Evidently he stretched a bit too long, and a man several rows back hollered, "Sit down you idiot!" The now-limbered stretcher turned and threatened, "Don't call me an idiot." Guess what happened next. Several security guards later, both men were excused from the arena. Might there possibly have been a more mature and effective way to deal with a seemingly harmless situation?

I employed this tack recently, with interesting results. I had been at a fast-food restaurant for a take-out order for my sons and me. I made the supreme mistake of not double-checking the order before leaving, and sure enough, when we began to eat, I realized I had been shorted part of my meal, which I had paid for of course. About an hour later, I had to drive near the same establishment, so I stopped in and showed them the wrapper from what they had given me, and explained that I had ordered and paid for more than that. The manager thanked me for pointing it out and said she was sorry. I said, "Not as sorry as I am since I paid for the more expensive meal." I was absolutely flabbergasted that they did not offer me any compensation, but I left quietly to plan my revenge.

Fortunately, I did not have to wait too many days, since some fast-food restaurants mess up orders with alarming regularity. This time I approached the manager and said, "Trade places with me for a minute. You are the customer and I am the manager. You received the wrong order, less than what you ordered and paid for. What would you like for me, the manager, to do for you?" She told me that she would like either a refund or an extra sandwich (the one she originally ordered). So I took the sandwich. Not only did I treat her in the respectful manner with which I would want her to treat me, but I allowed her to make the decision that she thought was fair from a customer point of view.

This concept becomes increasingly difficult to exercise on a consistent basis if status (real or imagined) is an issue. We have kind of an unwritten law in our society that respect goes from the bottom up, but not necessarily in the opposite direction. When was the last time your boss referred to you as Mr. or Mrs. or Miss, but you referred to him or her as John or Mary? Who rides in the front seat, the parents or the kids? When was the last time you had a ball player or a Hollywood personality ask for your autograph? Did you ever have your company President travel to <u>your</u> office for a meeting instead of having you trek to his or her office?

I witness this all the time with my adult students. They remark how amazed they are that they are treated like equal adults by our instructors. They are used to being treated as inferior people (peon students) by professors, some of whom are younger than they are. One of the concepts we discuss in class is the proper and improper use of power, and I use phrases like "position power" and "personal power" to emphasize the difference between them. Position power means that I have the title and/or authority, and on that basis I expect respect, whether or not I actually deserve it. Personal power means that I have the respect of others because of the kind of human being I am.

Personal power people do not have to hide behind titles or achievements or rank in order to be respected, admired, and esteemed. Typically, these people have mastered the art of the Relationship Rule, and they treat all other individuals as they would want to be treated by those others. Personal power doesn't go to one's head. In fact, the very word "power" might best be described as influence. These are the people you like because of who they are and what they stand for, not because of what position they hold. Personal power people possess true humility, as we described in the last chapter. They know their own strengths and weaknesses, and they recognize and admire the strengths of others. They have found a way to deal with others as they would like to be dealt with by others, regardless of standing, status, or other superficial differences.

> ### *"The more I know of people,*
> ### *the more I love my dog."*
> ### *– Anonymous*

Allow me to quickly share six very practical ideas for dealing with neighbors. These are in keeping with all the other concepts we have discussed in this book, and may help to turn potential negative encounters into positive ones, thus improving relationships. When you are in a position to influence or affect a neighbor negatively, fight the urge to simply react to the situation, and instead proactively choose to interact with him or her as you would want that individual to interact with you.

1. <u>When uncertain, give him or her the benefit of the doubt.</u>
   Don't assume the worst about the person, and then respond based on your assumption. As you would want to be treated fairly, do the same for your neighbor.

2. <u>When angry, speak the truth in love.</u>
   Don't spew words you will probably regret later. Maintain the open relationship by being truthful, but do it in a kind manner. Remember to use I-Statements.

3. <u>When tempted to insult, mentally trade places.</u>
   Is the insult you are about to use one that you would want someone to hurl at you? Will it effectively deal with the issue at hand, or just exacerbate the problem?

4. <u>When seeking revenge, look at the long-range picture.</u>
   What will be accomplished by achieving revenge? Will it solve the
   ultimate problem, or simply make you feel better for a few minutes?
   What further problems might it cause?

5. <u>When in conflict, think win-win.</u>
   Don't attempt to better your own situation at the expense of your
   neighbor. There are usually ways to resolve conflict so that both
   parties are content.

6. <u>When in a position to help, do so if possible.</u>
   Utilize the resources available to you to assist your neighbor.
   You will strengthen a relationship which will ultimately come
   back to benefit you.

The above suggestions are hardly profound, but the results can be. As an
interesting experiment, try to implement the six ideas in every encounter
you have with a neighbor for one week. I would be willing to bet that it
will be the best relational seven days you have experienced in a long
time. And there is a healthy side effect which probably will accompany
the experiment—reduction of stress. Many studies indicate that one of
the areas of our lives which produces the greatest amount of stress is
negative relationships we maintain with people, including spouses,
bosses, children, friends, and even strangers. Imagine how gloriously
boring it might be to go for one week without fighting with someone.
Ennui never sounded better.

> ### *If we all loved our neighbors,*
> ### *the six o'clock news*
> ### *would be a very short program.*

In 1945, a number of nations in the world recognized the need to treat
their neighbors with dignity and respect, to proactively join together to
preserve universal peace, to lessen the chances of incurring a third world
war. Part of the Preamble to the Charter of the United Nations reads like
this: "And for these ends to practice tolerance and live together in peace
with one another as good neighbors . . ."

How Naïve Can You Be?

Just so you don't think I have totally lost touch with reality, let me assert that I am well aware that not all people wish to be neighborly, and that in some cases, no matter what you do nor how hard you try, some people will steadfastly resist all attempts at civil behavior and relational activity. I wish that were not the case, but unfortunately it is. Whether it is due to ignorance, experience, personality, or just plain human nature, there will always be some people who will not cooperate relationally or allow you to be a good neighbor.

Defensiveness, mistrust, hatred, poor self-images, greed, and a myriad of other dysfunctional behaviors still abound in the world, and there is no panacea for maintaining good neighborly relations with everyone. I find it interesting that even _The Bible_, which advocates love for all neighbors at all times, allows that it is not always possible to control the relationship. It states, "If possible, so far as it depends on you, be at peace with all men." It goes on to warn against taking revenge, and it advocates loving your enemies, but it clearly admits that the two-way responsibility does not fall only on one person. You cannot force a relationship, and it is not your responsibility to do so.

> *"The most amiable man on earth can live*
> *at peace with his neighbor only*
> *as long as his neighbor chooses."*
> *– Anonymous*

So how do I deal with someone who I identify as a neighbor, but who is absolutely unreachable with regard to amicable relationships? How long must I try? How patient must I be? When can I quit? When do I finally get to tell the person how utterly obnoxious he or she really is? I have a quartet of suggestions:

First, be patient. Not all battles are won overnight. Some people take longer to come around than others. If I have lived my entire life in trusting relationships, and someone else has lived his entire life in abusive relationships (kind of an oxymoron), he will probably not be as quick a convert as I am to peaceful harmony. In addition, bad habits die hard. If Melanie has worked for years for bosses who have treated her as an inferior person, and who have always been quick to point out her faults but never her attributes, how will she tend to respond to Lois, her new boss, who tries to gently coach her and help her correct her mistakes? Lois will need to be patient with her new neighbor, Melanie, who probably possesses great potential. How would Lois like to be treated by her own boss?

Second, be proactive. This is the opposite of being reactive, and typically requires more than a modicum of maturity. That is why many people do not practice it—we have been subliminally immersed in the stimulus-response mode of behavior, and we have grown accustomed to it. As was mentioned in a previous chapter, "You make me angry" is a reactive response. Actually, no one can make me angry. I choose to be angry, but I blame it on you, as if I had no other option. As a mature individual, I recognize that if a "neighbor" treats me in a negative manner, I do not have to respond in kind. If I elect to do so, I can ignore, be amused by, or respond to his behavior. If he treats me poorly, I do not have to treat him poorly, although I may opt for that. I have choices, and one of them is to be consistent with my values, even if he does not share them.

Third, be principled. This follows closely on the heels of proactivity. I wish to live my life according to my values and principles. If I find myself in a situation where the behavior of others challenges or violates my values, I can speak the truth in love, or I can choose to remove myself from the encounter. This is not always easy, especially at the work place. But in a face-to-face encounter with a "neighbor" who obstinately refuses to accept or abide by the principles of effective communication, I retain the option of controlling my own behavior according to my values. I may be prone to operate outside of my value system in order to experience the euphoria of a "zinger," but in the grand scheme of things, I choose to abide by my principles, as they serve me well over the long haul.

Fourth, be prevailing. What I mean here is, learn when to walk away. A number of years ago, there was a popular song titled, "The Gambler." One of the refrain lines was, "You gotta know when to hold them, and know when to fold them." Despite the attempts at being patient, proactive, and principled, sometimes it just doesn't work. Sometimes the neighbor is incorrigible and the situation is helpless (please avoid the temptation to leap to this last step without trying the others first). At this point, you need to wash your hands of the situation, knowing that you did all that you could do. The results are out of your control, but you maintain your dignity and principles. It is an unfortunate fact of life, but we are not always in control. The wise person recognizes that, and exercises control over him or her self in all uncertainties.

One More Glance In The Mirror

It should come as no surprise to any of us that the more people like themselves, the more they tend to like others, and the more they dislike themselves, the more they tend to dislike others. The more secure they are in themselves, the more trusting they are of others. The less secure they are in themselves, the more critical they are of others. The more accepting they are of themselves, the more accepting they are of others. The more they have experienced love, the more love they have to offer to others. The more they realize all they have been forgiven for, the more forgiving they are toward others. It all comes back to healthy self-esteem and true humility.

There are reasons why some people like to criticize, judge, and hate, while others choose to accept people as they are, give the benefit of the doubt, and love whenever possible. There are reasons why some people elect to hold others up to their own standards, while other people attempt to walk a mile in the other's moccasins in an attempt to know what it is like to be that other person. There are reasons why some people can only feel good about themselves when they are tearing down their neighbors, and why some people feel so much better when they are uplifting their neighbors. There are reasons why some people continue to claim the title, Judge of the Universe, while others recoil from that awesome responsibility because of their own fallibility and lack of perfection.

> *"The better we feel about ourselves,*
> *the fewer times we have to knock*
> *somebody else down to feel tall."*
> *– Odetta*
> *(quoted in Quotable Quotes, p. 17)*

As we conclude this section on the THEMs in our lives, try to gain a realistic picture on where you are regarding your neighbors. Identify some THEMs in your life who challenge you in the area of acceptance and amiable relationships. Remind yourself what kinds of things you control and what kinds of things you don't control in those relationships. In some cases, it might serve you well to mend some fences and patch up some wounds. In other cases, it might be best to walk away and have as few dealings as possible. But the key is to do <u>something</u> that is proactive and positive, and not to continue feeding an unhealthy relationship.

There have been people in my life who I have had to mentally walk away from because I knew that it was ultimately fruitless to pursue a positive relationship, and I am sure that some others have felt the same way about me. What I have attempted to do, not always successfully, is to maintain respect for the person as a human being, regardless of our differences. If you cannot respect another person's values, work ethic, or treatment of others, then it is probably best to steer clear of that individual as much as is possible, while still attempting to respect his or her personhood.

"I never met a man I didn't like."
– Will Rogers

"Whoever said he never met a man
he didn't like never met my opponent."
– A political figure running for office

I would like to close this chapter, and this section of the book, by reconfirming my commitment to the THEMs in my life, especially those with whom I have contact. I believe my neighbor is anyone who I have the opportunity to influence or affect, either positively or negatively. In whatever way I can, with whatever resources I have available, I would like to treat my neighbor with dignity and respect, and as much as is possible, to live in peace with all people.

SUMMARY OF PART 4

In this section of the book, we have focused on the THEMs in our lives. These are people with whom we have no intimate relationship, whether we know them well or not at all. Therefore, there are close THEMs and distant THEMs. We have seen how, on the "HIT ME" active side, we should attempt to build relationships, communicate effectively, and commit to these individuals as appropriate. We have discussed how we owe them respect as fellow human beings.

On the "STAY" inactive side of the equation, we have understood how easy it is to set ourselves up as critics and judges when people do not share our values or attitudes. We have seen how easy it is to fall into the trap of nominating ourselves as Judge of the Universe. We have discovered that most of our critical natures emanate from arrogance, assumptions, and lack of true humility. We have investigated five very practical ways to reduce or eliminate our tendencies toward unfair judgment of others. We have reminded ourselves that if we do not really understand and appreciate our own selves, then it is easy to be critical of the behavior of others—we need to turn the microscope into a mirror in order to examine our own imperfections, and worry less about the blemishes of others.

We have investigated the assertion that my neighbor is anyone who I have the opportunity to influence or affect, either positively or negatively. We have identified a great many of these neighbors, and discussed how the Relationship Rule might assist us in effectively dealing with them for mutual benefit. We have observed how being patient, proactive, principled, and prevailing might be of assistance as we interact positively with all the neighbors in our lives. We concluded by reconfirming our commitment to love our neighbors as ourselves.

The final brief section of this book, CONCLUSION, is very critical as it attempts to wrap up our study of relationships. I trust you will read it carefully and thoughtfully, and make it intensely personal.

CONCLUSION

♦♦♦

"Look backward, step forward"

I have chosen to call this section **Conclusion** instead of Chapter 13, in deference to all of you trichadecaphobics in the crowd. My purpose here is very simple and straightforward—to ask you to join with me in making a commitment to live out the principles discussed in this book. Please do not gloss over this section just because it is the last one. It is in my opinion the most important one in the entire book, and yet it would be meaningless without the first 12 chapters. This is a call to action, and I hope you will travel with me down this difficult, yet ecstatically rewarding, road.

"What was most significant about the lunar voyage was not that men set foot on the moon but that they set eye on the earth."
– Norman Cousins
(quoted in Quotable Quotes, *p. 22)*

I am going to ask you to do something very difficult, and perhaps a bit awkward. Try to step outside of yourself emotionally while remaining within yourself intellectually. In other words, attempt to view yourself as objectively as possible, without bias or prejudice. As man set foot on the moon and gazed back at the only home he had ever known, try to remove yourself from the only person you have ever known, and look at yourself as another person might look at you.

As you address the following questions, answer them as honestly as you can, not as you "wish" were the case. Since you are scoring this yourself, you have two advantages. First, you don't have to share your answers with anyone and second, you can set the "passing score" bar anywhere you want. I say that with tongue in cheek, but I have a suggestion. If you are serious about this, after you have responded to the questions, talk about those responses with a special YOU in your life, and ask him or her to validate or negate your answers. That kind of feedback might open up some eyes which have been subject to tunnel vision for way too long. Speak the truth in love to both yourself and your special YOU.

ME

1. How accurate is my understanding of myself in terms of my abilities, limitations, attitudes, goals, honesty, and temperament?

2. Do I regularly take the time to reflect on who I really am, and concentrate on continuously improving myself?

3. What is one significant step I have taken in the past 6 or 12 months in an effort to grow as a person?

YOU

1. Since beginning to read this book, what is one concrete way in which I have changed my perception of a special YOU in my life?

2. What is one area of temperament difference that I still find to be difficult to handle, and how can I best attempt to improve my understanding?

3. What are the 1 or 2 points along the STOP sign that I continue to struggle with, and what plan do I have to experience growth in those areas?

US

1. In one special intimate relationship in my life, what is my progress like regarding being feeling, fueling, feeding, and forthright?

2. When speaking with a special YOU, do I tend to be more truthful (and less loving) or more loving (and less truthful)? How can I better achieve an appropriate balance?

3. As I probingly reflect, do I have any relationships with YOUs that are not as healthy as I desire (crutch, convenience, companion)? How can I best "re-relate?"

THEM

1. What is one relationship problem I currently have with a THEM in my life which I wish could be corrected? What is my first step in that process?

2. Do I tend to be critical or judgmental of those I do not really know or understand? What is one practical step I can take to resign as Judge of the Universe?

3. Is there someone who needs me to be a Good Samaritan? How can I best focus my attention on practicing the Relationship Rule with all the THEMs in my life?

Each one of the questions above addresses a significant area of relationships all of us experience in our lives. In every case, there are actions we can take to cultivate or improve those relationships, if we choose to do so. Two thoughts you might want to consider—first, "if we choose to do so" is a key phrase. There has to be a serious willingness to want to strengthen (or patch up) a relationship. If the desire is not there, then that is okay, but let's not pretend that it is and make a half-hearted attempt to improve. What happens then is that we expect failure, subconsciously gear our efforts toward that failure, and then triumphantly express, "See, I knew it wouldn't work."

Second, if the desire is truly there, please remember that meaningful change takes time as well as effort. Very few overnight miracles take place, which is probably a good thing. "Easy come, easy go" is still a viable concept, and what appears gift-wrapped and cheap typically is not a positive thing for the duration. Positive change is a process which can take days, weeks, months, or even years, but the continuous growing which accompanies that process provides numerous benefits along the way, and often opens even more doors that we did not know existed. It has come to my attention recently that Rome was not built in a day. Well, neither are relationships, but if today is better than yesterday, and if I learn something today which will make tomorrow even better, then I like the direction this thing is taking.

Two Steps Forward, One Step Back

I want to add a note of caution and encouragement here. It is human nature to get excited about something, verbally "commit" to it, try it out, and when the first failure experience comes along, dump it. American businesses have been doing this for years with regard to employee training programs. Business leaders read or hear about a concept for empowerment or employee inclusion, spend thousands or millions of dollars to research it, develop it, and implement it, and then at the first snafu, they trash it and return to the safety of the bureaucratic hierarchy.

This will not be of much comfort, but let me assure you that as you commit to the relationship principles we have discussed in this book, you will fail numerous times. I can assert this with confidence because I have never known anyone who did not experience some failures while attempting to improve his or her relational style. I continue to experience failures on a regular basis, and I want to kick myself every time. Here is the key point. If I concentrate on the failures and frustrations, I will continue to fail and eventually I will quit trying. If I use the failures as learning experiences and concentrate on the growth pattern, I will continue to get better.

A mediocre baseball batter determines he wants to be a very good hitter, so what does he do? He takes extra batting practice, he talks to other good hitters about their attitudes and styles, and he studies them when they are at bat. Eventually, he begins to hit better. But then he goes into a slump, and he has two choices. He can say to himself, "I guess I am just a mediocre hitter and I will never be any better, so why am I wasting all this time taking batting practice?" Or he can accept the fact that at this point he is struggling, but re-commit to his goal of being a good hitter, and try even harder than ever before to practice and get help wherever he can find it. That is the difference between a player who will have a long baseball career and a player who will seek another occupation in a relatively short period of time.

As we attempt to improve our relationships, we can expect failures along the way, and we need to welcome them as opportunities for growth and learning. We then need to re-commit ourselves to the YOUs and the THEMs in our lives, as well as to our goal of becoming better relational partners. It helps to have teammates here—YOUs who will understand our frailties, love us anyway, and encourage us to "keep on keeping on." Please don't let set-backs derail your growth train. The benefits and rewards make the effort worth it.

True Humility

As strongly as I can, I want to emphasize something I mentioned in an earlier chapter because I believe it is the absolute crux of developing and maintaining positive relationships with all the YOUs and THEMs in our lives. This is the concept of true humility. If you recall, I defined humility as having an accurate picture of who I am, not thinking too highly of myself, nor too lowly. It is understanding my strengths and weaknesses, and appreciating the strengths and weaknesses of others. It is thinking of myself as equal to all other human beings, not greater or less. I am no more important or special than the prisoner on death row, and I am no less important or special than a famous movie personality or a world leader. I am not as powerful or wealthy or intelligent as many other people, but in the grand scheme of humanity, I am just as important and special. True humility is the understanding that every human being is on a level playing field in terms of his or her personhood.

"Once the game is over, the king and the pawn go back into the same box."
– Italian proverb
(quoted in Quotable Quotes, p. 203)

The reason I am re-emphasizing this point is that if we can consciously practice true humility in our everyday lives, we will eliminate the vast majority of our relationship problems. If we view the individuals with whom we interact on a regular basis as true equals in every respect, it will radically alter the way we do business, discuss issues, resolve conflicts, and treat each other.

- We will no longer look up to the wealthy and down on the poor.
- We will no longer allow "social status" to dictate the way we deal with others.

- We will no longer allow power to go to our heads, and think that others are there to serve us.
- We will no longer be critical of people who dress differently, talk differently, act differently, or communicate differently from the way we do.
- We will no longer benignly assume that our way of doing everything is the right way, and that everyone else is out of step with the beat we have established.
- We will no longer be tempted to judge people whose lives we have not lived, nor whose experiences we have not experienced.

This is so easy to talk about, and so hard to do. Every time I begin a new group of adult students, on the very first night of class I have them develop a list of expectations for the group, since they will spend the next 14 months together. Every group I have ever taught has included in their list of expectations, "To be respectful of each other and to listen to what everyone has to say." Sounds great, doesn't it?

But in far too many groups, after a number of weeks, certain people identify the class "dummies," those who are less intelligent or less sophisticated, those who have had inferior formal education and express themselves in a less refined manner than others do. Then I see the eyes roll, and I hear the snickers, and it breaks my heart because here is someone struggling to complete college, and doing the best he or she can, and others have appointed themselves as Judges of the Universe, and choose to criticize someone who may not possess all the communication skills they do. When I observe this, it angers me, but then it also causes me to reflect on my own attitude toward other people. How quick I am to judge someone else, and think that I am superior.

When I am in a fast-food restaurant with my sons (which is a common occurrence because that is what they like, and it costs their father less money than a sit-down restaurant), sometimes our order is taken by someone for whom English is a second language. When the order is misunderstood or comes out wrong, I get frustrated and am tempted to shout, "Why don't you hire people who speak English?"

Then I think about the person taking the order, and I realize that he or she had no choice as to place of origin or language learned, that he or she is responsible enough to have a job, and that he or she is deserving of my respect because we are both human beings. It changes my perspective on how to act toward fellow individuals. What right do I have to be haughty or superior because I have had more fortunate circumstances in my life than others have had? What right do I have to be arrogant, and less than humble? *The Bible* declares, "God opposes the proud, but gives grace to the humble." I want that kind of grace in my life. I want to know that I am doing everything I can to influence or affect other people as positively as I can.

> ***"There is no king who has not had a slave among his ancestors, and no slave who has not had a king among his."***
> *– Helen Keller*
> *(quoted in <u>Quotable Quotes</u>, p. 53)*

Have you ever seen the bumper sticker, "He who dies with the most toys wins?" I realize it is meant to be humorous, not to mention making money for whoever produced it, but it has always bothered me. I would rather see, "He or she who dies with the most precious relationships wins" or "He or she who dies having left a legacy of relational living wins." I have often thought about what I want my twin boys to be able to say about me after I am dead, and I think I can summarize it this way: "Dad loved us unconditionally as much as a father can love, and he taught us to love God and other people." That is a legacy I can live (and die) with.

Two Personal Reflections

As I bring this book to a close, I would like to share with you two personal reflections, which are closely tied together. The first is this—as I stated in the Introduction, and in several other places in the book, I do not pretend to have all the answers regarding effective relationships. I am a fellow struggler with you, seeking continuous growth in my life. But I see that as a good thing, not a bad thing. Growth is like maturity, potential, and self-actualization. If anyone thinks that he or she has achieved it, that is the first sign that he or she is deluded.

Relational growth is a never-ending process, and if it is not on-going, it is not alive. We cannot speak about having grown, only growing. We cannot speak about reaching maturity, only maturing. We cannot speak about being self-actualized, only the process of continuous self-actualizing. I wish I had a corner on the market of relational truth, but I do not. I have merely shared some ideas with you that I have found helpful in my own struggles, and I sincerely hope that some of them might be helpful for you also.

Second, it has occurred to me during the 18 months of writing this book, that it has been a great deal more beneficial for me than it will have been for you. Writing this has encouraged me to reexamine my life in ways that I never did before. It has caused me to re-assess my values, beliefs, attitudes, and actions. It has assisted me in changing some behavioral patterns in my life, and attempting to alter some paradigms in my mind and heart. It has significantly changed the way I think about certain individuals, and treat the YOUs and THEMs in my life. It has helped me to put into perspective the values and priorities I hold dear. Above all, it has gently persuaded me to make certain commitments in my life, and this is where I urge you to join me.

Let's commit together that we will be less critical, suspicious, un-accepting, and judgmental of others in our lives. Let's commit together that we will be more loving, accepting, humble, and relational. Let's commit together that we will minimize our negative feelings toward ourselves and others, and that we will maximize our abilities to be positive, nurturing, and loving in all the relationships we encounter in our lives. Let's commit to internalizing the ideas of positive and effective relational living. Let's commit to both the <u>People</u> and the <u>Principles</u> as we attempt to strengthen our relationships, in order to make them healthier, more meaningful, and a more significant part of our lives. Let's commit to being **REAL** with each other. In that context, I want to conclude with this excerpt from one of my favorite books, _The Velveteen Rabbit_ (pages 16-17). It is a story of stuffed animals and other playthings residing in the toy box of a young boy, and the conversation takes place between a rabbit and a skin horse.

"What is REAL?" asked the Rabbit one day, when they were lying side by side near the nursery fender, before Nana came to tidy the room. "Does it mean having things that buzz inside you and a stick-out handle?"

"Real isn't how you are made," said the Skin Horse. "It's a thing that happens to you. When a child loves you for a long, long, time, not just to play with, but REALLY loves you, then you become real."

"Does it hurt?" asked the Rabbit.

"Sometimes," said the Skin Horse, for he was always truthful. "When you are Real you don't mind being hurt."

"Does it happen all at once, like being wound up," he asked, "or bit by bit?"

"It doesn't happen all at once," said the Skin Horse. "You become. It takes a long time. That's why it doesn't often happen to people who break easily, or have sharp edges, or who have to be carefully kept. Generally, by the time you are Real, most of your hair has been loved off, and your eyes drop out and you get loose in the joints and very shabby. But those things don't matter at all, because once you are Real you can't be ugly, except to people who don't understand."